Oral History

Oral History

AN INTRODUCTION FOR STUDENTS

by
James Hoopes

The University of North Carolina Press
Chapel Hill

Manufactured in the United States of America

99 98 97 96 95 11 10 9 8 7

Library of Congress Cataloging in Publication Data

Hoopes, James, 1944–
Oral history.

Bibliography: p.
Includes index.
1. Oral history. I. Title.
D16.14.H66 907 78-9956
ISBN 0-8078-1341-9
ISBN 0-8078-1344-3 pbk.

For Alice Armstrong

When, in talk with a friend, you tell him or hear from him, details of childhood, those details are perhaps even more real to you than in your solitary memory; and they are real and exciting to both of you in a way no form of art can be, or anyhow is. He is accepting what you say as truth, not fiction. You in turn, and the truth you are telling, are conditioned in some degree by his personality—you are in part, and he knows you are in part, selecting or inventing toward his color—but your whole effort, at which you both may be willing and interested to spend a great deal of time, is to reduce these half-inventions more and more towards the truth. The centrally exciting and important fact, from which ramify the thousand others which otherwise would have no clear and valid existence, is: that was the way it was. What could be more moving, significant or true: every force and hidden chance in the universe has so combined that a certain thing was the way it was.

James Agee,
Let Us Now Praise Famous Men

Contents

PART ONE

1

History and Oral History

Too often we forget that history is, among other things, an exercise of the imagination. History, like life, is a test of our ability imaginatively to place ourselves in the positions of other people, so that we can understand the reasons for their actions. Through research and study we learn facts about those other people. But we can never know everything about anyone, living or dead. The historical record is always incomplete. Imagination must fill in the gaps in our knowledge, though of course our imaginings must derive from facts and be consistent with them. Dependence on imagination is characteristic of all study of human behavior, including, for example, psychology or sociology. But in history there is the added problem that the people we hope to understand lived in other times and may therefore be more remote from us than people in foreign lands today. Only through superior acts of the imagination can we hope to understand people so removed from ourselves.

Because history is an act of our minds, historical knowledge can lead to self-knowledge. To test or verify historical thought we must check not only the data or facts but also our thinking itself. We therefore learn not only about history but about the quality of our minds. This process is no different from that followed in the exact sciences, except that the qualities revealed in historical thinking include those of human and imaginative sympathy. Biases, prejudices, predispositions, all manner of attitudes and likes and dislikes, which we may not even have known we had, are revealed when we study a discipline like history, with its human content. History should be one of the most interesting, personally challenging, of all disciplines.

Yet students have been voting with their feet in recent years, and enrollment in history courses has declined sharply. Partly, this decline may be the result of economic circumstances and the need students feel for practical, useful knowledge that will help them start careers. But partly, too, it may be the result of history's having become a much more technical discipline than it once was: for students, technics may have obscured history's human content. Historians have been exploring numerous kinds of new techniques and theories, but the danger of sacrificing the end for the means is perhaps especially great with the quantitative methods that now interest many, though still a minority, of them. Most quantitative historians have surely not forgotten that we not only must know the facts but also must imagine what the facts meant to the human beings who lived them. But the lengthy, sometimes tedious nature of quantitative research points up the need for all teachers of history to remember that, for you who are students, history must be a means to a human end now, not years from now when your course work is far behind you.

If what is interesting in historical work is its personal, human challenge, one way to keep it interesting is to focus directly on human beings. This book's purpose is to acquaint you with a method of historical research—oral history—that is necessarily a human challenge, because it involves direct personal contact with other people. Such research is a test of other people, of the accuracy of their memories, of their ability to assess their own lives realistically, and of their ability to profit from experience. In a sense it is a test of other people as historians, a test of how well they can deal with their personal histories. But oral history research is also a test of ourselves, of our ability to deserve and win the confidence of other people, of our ability to deal sympathetically but honestly and imaginatively with their memories, and of our ability to deal honestly with ourselves. All these tests are involved also, if not always so obviously, in more traditional historical research. Oral history is therefore good training for other kinds of history and may be a path to a greater understanding of ourselves and others, including not only those alive now but also those who have ceased to live except in our imaginations.

Things that have survived from the past, called documents, are the basis of historical knowledge. Most historians rely on written documents, such as books, letters, diaries, deeds, census and tax records, church registers, bills of lading, and so on. But houses, coins, tools, gravestones, furniture, and folklore or legends handed down from generation to generation are also documents and can tell us much about the people who created them. This last sort of document, folklore or legend, differs from the others in that it has its origins in speech. Oral history is based on documents that are spoken, and folklore and legend are only one kind of spoken document. Songs, speeches, interviews, and formal and informal conversation are all oral documents, useful for history.

Documents are only useful for history if they are in some

way preserved. Material documents, such as houses, letters, and coins, would seem more likely to be preserved than intangible speech, which vanishes into the air. But some kinds of speech, including folklore, legend, and song, are preserved by memory and later spoken again to the next generation. In illiterate societies there are often found more or less professional storytellers (or historians) whose task is to learn the story of the past from elders and then pass it on to the next generation. Such oral documents are the basis of much of *Roots*, the famous book in which Alex Haley traces his slave ancestors back to Africa. Though there is controversy about the accuracy of Haley's oral research in Africa, such documents can be accurate and useful and are in any case the only verbal sources about the history of many peoples.

"Oral tradition" is the usual name for these verbal stories passed on from one generation to the next. It is commonly accepted that in literate societies like the United States oral tradition is not as reliable as in illiterate societies, where people are well practiced in remembering stories, where story telling is highly ritualized, and where the teller may even be punished for changing the story's form or content.[1] Yet in the United States, research in oral tradition may be useful in dealing with particular or local cultures, such as those of native and black Americans, who may not be literate or may have been denied a written history because of political oppression. It is a powerful testimony to the usefulness of oral tradition in black history that Alex Haley's grandmother taught him both the name of his great-great-great-great-grandfather, who first came to America as a slave, and also the name of that slave ancestor's first master. It is a

1. Jan Vansina, *Oral Tradition*, pp. 6, 15.

powerful testimony also to the possible accuracy of oral tradition, because both names were later verified by research in written documents.[2] Anyone wishing to do research in oral tradition should consult the best book on the subject, *Oral Tradition: A Study in Historical Methodology*, by Jan Vansina.

But the focus here, in this book, is on "oral history" in a much more restricted sense, a sense that is more useful in a generally literate country without a strong oral tradition. Rather than the collecting of stories handed down from generation to generation, "oral history" will here refer to the collecting of any individual's spoken memories of his life, of people he has known, and events he has witnessed or participated in. Collecting even these personal, firsthand, fairly immediate memories and checking their accuracy require great care in a society that depends on written records and does not much exercise its memory.

Furthermore, because of the invention of electronic sound-recording equipment, memory in literate societies is exercised even less frequently than only a few years ago. Before the invention of sound recording, the preservation of spoken words depended mainly on memory, which might later have been preserved in writing. This was sometimes true even of important public addresses, such as Abraham Lincoln's famous "Lost Speech," supposedly so great that every reporter present forgot to take notes and instead listened raptly. One of Lincoln's biographers, Ida Tarbell, recovered a sketchy account of the speech forty years later from a member of Lincoln's audience still living then. But in recent years the tape recorder has reduced the degree to which we must rely

2. Alex Haley, "Black History, Oral History and Genealogy," p. 24.

on memory to preserve not only speeches but also, sometimes unfortunately, conversations. Surely the most famous tape-recorded conversations in history are those between ex-President Nixon and his aides. They are certain to be of great interest and novelty to historians, who have usually had to rely on less direct evidence to learn what goes on in the White House.

Oral history's first interviews were recorded manually, but without the invention of the tape recorder, oral history might not have become the veritable movement that it is today. Some oral historians, a minority, would even limit the use of the term "oral history" to documents collected by tape recorder.[3] Nevertheless, we will keep our definition centered on the oral nature of the document rather than on the technique used to record it. If you do not have access to a tape recorder, this book will suggest a way to do oral history by taking written notes.

Oral documents are also used by social scientists in "participant observation" studies, in which the social scientist is on the scene, participating in the action he records, rather than asking someone else to recall it later. An example is Thomas J. Cottle's fine book, *Busing*, about school desegregation in Boston. Although Cottle does not ignore the past, his principal objective is to understand what people are feeling now. Such studies are often called "oral history," and the designation makes sense; they are oral and will probably be useful documents for future historians. But the distinction between recording "on the scene" and recording spoken

3. Gould P. Colman, "Oral History—An Appeal for More Systematic Procedures," p. 80. For useful comments on the disadvantages of the tape recorder for the oral historian, see Saul Benison, "Oral History."

memories ought to be kept clear.[4] Participant observation is outside the scope of this book. "Oral history" will here refer to spoken memories. The major difference between the two types of research is that the participating observer has the advantage of being at (or in) the scene his subjects speak about. The oral historian cannot visit the scene the interviewee remembers, at least not until the time machine is perfected. To overcome this disadvantage, the oral historian must do careful background research, which is the subject of chapter 7.

It is often asserted that recording spoken memories has become especially important because of the communications revolution in this century. According to this line of reasoning, people living now, whether statesmen or ordinary citizens, are much less likely than their forebears of a hundred years ago to leave historians written documents, at least of an intimate sort. Where people once wrote to friends or business associates and saved the answering letters to read a second time, they now talk on the telephone, and no written record survives. Diaries have suffered a fate similar to that of letters, perhaps not only because television and other distractions of modern life allow less time for them, but also because people who no longer have to write so much do not write so well or eagerly as they once did. Yet thanks to the tape recorder, people who once would have left letters and diaries behind them can now leave spoken autobiographies. Thus, what the communications revolution has taken away it has also restored, in the form of tape-recorded interviews.

This generally correct line of reasoning should not become

4. As a rule, the recording of an occurrence will be found in a "sound archive," whereas recordings of spoken memories are filed in "oral history collections."

a rationale for not doing research in written records, which are definitely not falling into short supply. Writers, politicians, entertainers, and public figures of all kinds are donating their papers and memorabilia to libraries at an unprecedented rate. Sometimes a person has hardly emerged into prominence before a library tries to acquire his present and future papers. Under this sort of arrangement, when a person does not have to save his papers himself but can simply pass them on to a library for filing, the number of papers saved is likely to be greater than ever before. And the computerization of record keeping by business and government suggests that written or, rather, magnetically recorded statistical information about great numbers of people may be available in overwhelming proportions to future social historians. Yet although care is necessary in generalizing about the decline of written documents, it is probably true that some of this massive amount of material will be less revealing and useful to historians than previous written records.

This lack, unfortunately, cannot be completely made up by tape-recording spoken memories. No retrospective interview will ever recover what might have gone into an intimate letter or diary if the telephone or television had not prevented it from being written. Furthermore, anyone who has not only collected oral materials but worked them into a finished historical account will attest that oral history is most useful when written records are also available. Checking one sort of information against the other is an excellent method of verification. (But when there is a conflict between written and oral documents, it is not always the oral testimony that is unreliable. Occasionally, oral history will cast a new light on written records and prove them false or at least show that they must be interpreted in a new way.)

Although oral history cannot fully compensate for the loss of intimate written documents, it can sometimes supply information that might otherwise never have been saved. In Latin America, for instance, there is an aversion to autobiography, apparently based on the belief that it is undignified and egotistical to take the initiative in talking about oneself. The initiative must come from someone else, and as a result oral historians have become instrumental in saving the personal accounts of national leaders there.[5] Illicit and illegal behavior in any society is seldom recorded in writing, and as sociologists have long known, interviewing is one of the best ways of learning about it. Thus, oral history research has shown that birth control may have been far more widely practiced in the early years of this century than was once thought.[6] The often covert and extralegal tactics of racial and political oppressions, such as those to which American blacks have been subjected, make oral history a good technique for researching such subjects. One of the greatest writers in the world today, Alexander Solzhenitsyn, might fairly be called an oral historian, because *The Gulag Archipelago*, his trilogy on the Soviet Union's forced labor camps, is based on the spoken accounts of his fellow prisoners, who could not safely have written their stories. Even the politics of relatively open societies, though a traditional historical topic, are never completely documented in writing. T. Harry Williams, who used oral history extensively in his Pulitzer Prize-winning biography *Huey Long*, found that "the politicians were astonishingly frank in detailing their dealings, and often completely realistic in viewing themselves. But they had not

5. James W. Wilkie, *Elitelore*, p. 55.
6. Sherna Gluck, ed., *From Parlor to Prison*, p. 15.

trusted a word of these dealings to paper. . . . Anybody who heard them would have to conclude that the full and inside story of politics is not in *any* age committed to the [written] documents."[7] The point, then, is that oral history is not a substitute for written records but a complement to them.

The greatest advantage of oral over written documents is that the historian actively participates, as interviewer, in creating the oral document, and therefore he can try to get the information he needs. This active role for the historian can also be a great disadvantage, because if he does not guard against his biases, he may consciously or unconsciously fabricate the document and make it say what he wants it to say. But the very desirable goal of impartiality should never be confused with passivity. The best oral historians actively apply the criterion of usefulness in choosing interviewees and the subjects about which they are to be questioned. It might be argued that "usefulness" can mask many biases, but it can and should also stand for the use of intelligence to recognize those biases and reduce their influences as much as possible. It might also be argued against the oral historian's active role that no one knows what the viewpoint of future scholars will be and that information which now appears *useless* to us may be valuable someday. But information which now appears *useful* to us may also be valuable someday. Given that not everything can be preserved and that no one knows what the needs of the future will be, the best criterion of what should be saved is what we think should be saved. If future scholars use the information in ways unexpected to us, that is their affair. Meanwhile, we have not only the right but the obligation to use our minds and to maintain the active role that is the chief advantage of oral history.

7. P. ix.

Another way in which oral history can complement written documents is by encouraging and enabling the ordinary as well as the famous citizen to leave an autobiographical account of his life. Oral records can be similarly useful for prominent people who are too busy to write or whose talents lie along other lines. Probably none of the musicians whose narratives are printed in Art Hodes and Chadwick Hansen's *Selections from the Gutter: Portraits from the Jazz Record* would have written autobiographies, yet their stories are important. Oral histories of either ordinary persons or unlettered celebrities also show that, contrary to the gloomy prognostications of cultural critics, English is still expressively and vigorously spoken by at least some people.

Because oral history can be used to study ordinary people as well as the elite, it is sometimes asserted that it is an especially democratic form of research. There is something to this idea, but, again, qualification is necessary. Keeping in mind that oral history works best as a complement to written documents, it is obvious that it will be easiest to use to research people—usually the elite—about whom written records are preserved. Oral history can be used to study ordinary people, and that is a great virtue; but in the absence of written records it will require much more work, probably in the form of more numerous, lengthy, and detailed interviews, to place the oral accounts in a meaningful cultural and social context. Without that extra work, such interviews are likely to have little historical significance.

The need for context can easily be seen in *Hard Times: An Oral History of the Great Depression*, by the most popular oral historian, Studs Terkel. Actually, there is a certain unfairness in thinking of Terkel as an oral *historian* and judging his work by historical standards. He is a journalist working in the documentary tradition, and in *Hard Times* he was at least as much interested in the spirit with which people spoke at the time he did his interviewing as he was in the depression. That is a fine interest but that it is not history must be clear to any critical reader of the book. Except for the information in the more than one hundred interviews themselves and the order in which Terkel arranges them, no attempt is made to relate the individual experiences of either famous or ordinary interviewees to the experience of anyone else. Few immediate contexts are established, only the enormous and already given context of the depression. The result is that despite the often interesting and pungent words of the interviewees, we do not learn much more about the depression than we already knew from the popular images of soup lines and hobo villages. In a subsequent and much better book, *Working: People Talk About What They Do All Day and How They Feel About What They Do*, Terkel's interviews, again, lack context. But the often bitter narratives in this later book have a clearer, more powerful meaning simply because there is no mistaking that they are about the present. Despite the risk of unfairness to Terkel, comparing *Hard Times* to *Working* illustrates the important point that interviewing, used alone, is more enlightening about the present than the past. The oral *historian* must not only engage in interviewing but must also do other sorts of research in order to imaginatively recreate the historical context to which the interview refers and without which it will not often have much meaning.

Terkel, a Chicago radio talk show host, has also been criticized by academic oral historians because of his interviewing and editing techniques.[8] Academics say that he interviews to

8. Some of Terkel's critics are quoted succinctly by Joseph Roddy in "Oral History," pp. 2, 4.

get the information he wants and lets his biases and preconceptions interfere with the results. It is not clear how they draw this conclusion from his published work, because his questions printed there seem neutral enough. But one reads very few of his questions, for Terkel considerably edits and shortens the transcripts, usually omitting his own words. Some view this practice as a heresy and call it "Terkelism." It is certainly to be hoped that Terkel has saved his tapes and transcripts, so that the question of how well his edited selections represent entire interviews can be settled. But quoting selected passages to make a point is standard practice by historians, and Terkel's critics might be on solider ground if they lamented his apparent lack of interest in written documents and in establishing the cultural and social context without which his interviews often lack historical significance.

In addition to the question of meaningful context, oral historians must also deal with the problem that memory, on which they so heavily depend, is human and fallible. All historical documents, including both oral and written, reflect the particular subjective minds of their creators. Yet written records that date from the time of an event, though not less subjective, are at least less distorted by memory and therefore, some historians have argued, a better source of "facts" than oral documents. What oral history does best, according to this line of thought, is give a "feel" for the "facts" that "can be provided only by one who lived with them . . . ."[9] But feelings are also facts, at least in the historical sense, and the lapse of time can and does obscure a person's memory of what he felt in the past. There have been a number of psychological experiments suggesting that feelings (or inner facts)

9. John Rae, "Commentary," p. 175.

are less likely to be remembered accurately than external facts.[10] Common sense psychology supports this conclusion, because our feelings, even more than our outer behavior, are extremely personal facts, potentially most damaging to our egos when confronted honestly.

Historians, however, should be accustomed to using imperfect sources. Arriving at a general conclusion about what oral history does best is not as important as understanding how to minimize its defects in the various situations where it might contribute to knowledge. Where written documents are a good source of external facts but weak on feelings, the astute oral historian does more than merely use background research to test the accuracy of the interviewee's memory. In that case he uses research in written records in order to aid and cooperate in accurately recreating the past, to help the interviewee better remember both the facts and how he felt about them. Where there are few written documents or none at all, critical techniques must be devised for getting external facts from oral accounts. In *The Saga of Coe Ridge*, an oral history of a gory feud between blacks and whites in the hill country of southern Kentucky, William Lynwood Montell has convincingly argued for and demonstrated the possibility of writing local history on the basis of oral documents. Though details of an event are often reported incorrectly, says Montell, it is still possible, by collecting and collating numerous accounts, to get at the core of truth in all of them.[11]

A good example of these points can be found in one of the historically stronger sections of Terkel's *Hard Times*, which contains interviews of several people from the vicinity of Le

10. William W. Cutler III, "Accuracy in Oral Interviewing," p. 2.
11. Pp. 194–95.

Mars, Iowa, where a judge was threatened with lynching because of his quickness to foreclose farm mortgages. The details differed according to who was telling the story. Did members of the crowd, as one man said, only shake a rope in front of the judge's face, or did they, as others said, put a noose around his neck? Was it on the courthouse steps, or did they drag him off to the fairgrounds? Did they tar and feather him? Though one cannot answer these questions of detail, it is clear that the judge was threatened. And all the accounts make clear the feeling, the frustration, that led to such drastic action.

This evidence supports business historian John Rae's idea that oral history *can* help provide knowledge of the inner feelings that "are precisely what the historian must have to explain the 'why' as well as the 'how'. . . . "[12] Subjectivity, which, if distorted by memory, is a potential weakness of the oral document, can also be its strength. If the historian uses oral memoirs with at least as much care as he would a written autobiography, he can get about the same quality of information or perhaps better in some respects. We are likely to be more spontaneous in talking about our feelings than in writing about them, and many people speak to the oral historian with great candor and courage. These spoken memories and ruminations are the essential human stuff of our time, for they reveal inner sources and motives.

In order to preserve as many such documents as possible, oral historians have focused on the important task of collecting tape-recorded interviews, often conducted with old people before their memories are permanently lost. State and local history societies, universities, foundations, museums,

12. Rae, "Commentary," p. 175.

and businesses have organized, at last count, more than four hundred oral history projects involving literally thousands of staff members and tens of thousands of interviews. But there is more to oral history than the collection of raw interviews for the use of future scholars. As with all other documents, recorded interviews are not history until they have been interpreted by the historical imagination. It is our job as historians to take advantage of all sources available now, and the purpose of this book is to suggest ways not only of collecting oral documents but also of using them.

Using such documents is excellent training for living intelligently in contemporary society and culture, for documented nonfiction based on interviews has become a vital form of our literature. Such journalism as Tom Wicker's story of the Attica prison uprising in *A Time to Die*, such sociological studies as Michael Maccoby's analysis of the modern corporate executive in *The Gamesman*, and such detailed biographies of figures as diverse as Lennie Bruce and Eleanor Roosevelt all aim at presenting not only the external facts but also the inner feelings of their subjects. Nonfiction seems to be replacing the novel as our main resource for understanding human behavior, character, and personality.

Oral history in its more popular forms is part of this surge of interest in humanly interesting, documentary accounts of real people's lives. Many books of oral history have been published in recent years, and some of them have been best sellers—Terkel's *Hard Times*, for instance, and also Theodore Rosengarten's *All God's Dangers*, in which a solitary black Alabama tenant farmer wonderfully recounts his trials and triumphs.

But this popular new form of literature requires intelligent criticism and an alert audience if it is to achieve its best possible forms and greatest usefulness. And because many of the pertinent questions about books based on interviews are relevant to all oral history research, including yours, some of the discussions and examples in this book are drawn from published oral histories. My hope is that this book is an introduction not only to doing oral history research but also, even if only incidentally, to reading it. Such research and reading should be useful experience for those who wish better to understand themselves and the culture and society in which they live.

2

Oral History for the Student

Every good history course includes work meant to give you the experience of *doing* history. This is often a research paper, and it should be the most interesting, stimulating aspect of the course. Too often, though, it is tedious, not because it is hard work, but because the challenge to human sympathy and imagination is neglected. In part this may be because students sometimes feel that their efforts are repetitive, that they cannot do original research in documents that other historians and students have already researched. They are wrong to think so, because the test of originality, applied to history, is a test not only of the material's freshness or richness but also of the scholar's creativity. Still, this important point might be learned with more ease and interest if those of you who wished to work with new material could do so. One advantage of oral history interviewing as a teaching and learning technique is that the documents are always new, at least in the sense that no previous historian has examined them.

Some teachers, skeptical of the idea that students can profit from oral history research, might point out that history is an exercise not only of the imagination but also of the intellect. Oral history is so often thought of as merely the tape recording of interviews that it may seem a mindless activity to some. Actually, conducting a good interview requires hard intellectual as well as imaginative effort, just like other kinds of research. Yet an instructor who refuses to accept the raw tape or transcript of an interview is surely as much within his rights as he would be in refusing written research notes in place of a finished term paper. Though you are acting as a historian when doing research, your actions are not very visible. You are most clearly active as a historian when you can be seen thinking, rigorously and imaginatively, about your data. And a written research paper is usually the best way to reveal the quality of both your research and your thinking. This book is therefore designed around the idea that your oral history research will be incorporated into a more or less traditional term paper employing written documents as well.

At present, many students who have the opportunity to try oral history research do so in the context of a group oral history project. At their best, the student interviewers for these projects have a clear intellectual objective and use written documents as background material. The project at Duke University, for example, is focused on black history. Students participating in the project research written documents first and then use that research as a basis for conducting oral interviews, which become part of a permanent collection. In this way they have the satisfaction of knowing that they are contributing to a genuine scholarly purpose. I hope that this book will be useful to students in such projects.

But I have also designed this book for a larger audience

by suggesting that those of you who do not have the opportunity to participate in an oral history project can still use oral history in the term papers often assigned in upper division courses and sometimes in broader surveys as well. Oral history may comprise a large part or only a small portion of your research, depending on its usefulness for your particular topic. It is assumed that you already have some experience in doing library research. If not, you may wish to consult one of the numerous guides to writing term papers. *Researching and Writing in History*, by F. N. McCoy, is especially good on the biggest hurdle for many students—choosing a topic.

The objective of this book is to keep the clear intellectual focus of the best *group* oral history projects but to adjust some of their procedures to the needs of *individual* students and scholars. Students who wish to work with oral as well as written documents can do so (enthusiastically, I have found) in the context of the term paper. At the same time, other students are free to pursue different research interests and techniques. Though some class time may be devoted to oral history, most of the course can still be spent on whatever is supposed to be its subject—the history of business, labor, politics, science, society, and so on. Such freedom and flexibility in accommodating individual interests of both students and teachers are the only conditions under which oral history is likely to find broad acceptance in the classroom, especially the college classroom.

This attention to the needs of the individual researcher is consistent with the fact that this is the first "how to" book on oral history where "you" readers are students rather than teachers or researchers.[1] I follow as well as argue "trans-

1. John A. Neuenschwander, *Oral History as a Teaching Approach*, and Van Hastings Garner, *Oral History*, are addressed to teachers

actional" principles by acknowledging that students sometimes see teachers as destructively cautious in discouraging innovative research. But I also think that teachers are right to be skeptical of devoting an entire history course to *imitating* a group oral history project. It may be an excellent thing if the course is an *actual part* of an ongoing oral history project or if the course has a clear intellectual focus on a specific historical problem, with attention to background research and to preserving the interviews. But without that focus it is surely futile to import the conditions of a group project into the classroom by merely having students tape and transcribe interviews that, if the project is imitative, are unlikely ever to be used by anyone else. Taping and especially transcribing are too laborious to be done to no purpose.[2] You should be asked to engage in only the aspects of oral history that make sense for genuine historical or learning purposes. Otherwise, you will learn not history but the technique of oral history in a vacuum, and the result will be one more frustratingly sterile schoolroom exercise.

Addressing the needs of individual students engaged in individual projects is also consistent with an additional objective of this book—to address the problem of integrating oral history with other kinds of research and knowledge. Able students can and should make significant contributions to oral history, and I hope that this book, which I view as a

---

and follow the group approach. Cullom Davis et al., *Oral History,* though designed for possible use as a textbook, is not written especially for students.

2. Thomas Charlton reports, on the basis of a survey of college teachers, that "almost all universities face problems in motivating students to transcribe the results of their interviews" ("Oral History in Graduate Instruction," p. 66). In some cases the reluctance may be for good reason.

contribution to greater rigor and sophistication in the field of oral history, will help them to do so. My own qualifications for writing the book do not include experience as a professional oral historian, collecting for a group project. But I have used oral history techniques in my own research and am one of the numerous but nonetheless isolated teachers who have experimented with oral history in the classroom. Perhaps these are just the right qualifications for the author of a book addressed to the needs of individuals and to the question of how oral history can be related to other kinds of history.

Judging by much of the "how-to" literature, the field of oral history is at present relatively unsophisticated, not only in the obviously crucial area of interviewing, but perhaps more importantly in its relations with other types of historical research.[3] If oral history becomes an isolated field, more interested in the oral than the historical, it will not fulfill its potential for humanistic research. One professional oral historian has warned of "danger signs" that "A quasi-professional group called 'oral historians' might well emerge who become method-mad pedagogues, claiming authority on every facet of oral history. . . . Oral historians must be historians first."[4] The purpose of Part Two of this book is to suggest not only kinds of oral history research that you might do but even more importantly the need to give your research the broadest possible historical significance by placing it in cultural and social context.

3. Charlton found that integrating oral history with written sources was one of the most common difficulties reported by instructors using oral history as a teaching technique ("Oral History," p. 66).

4. Ramon I. Harris et al., *The Practice of Oral History*, pp. 76–77.

Concern for theoretical rigor should be an aid to doing research, not an excuse for delaying it. I have therefore tried to help get you involved in your own research as quickly as possible by writing the four parts of this book so that they can be read not only quickly but also independently of one another. If time presses and interviewing must begin soon, it should be possible to skip Part Two (not permanently, I hope) and go immediately to Part Three, where I have summarized some of the ideas of sociologists and communications specialists who have been most thoughtful about the problematic nature of information acquired by interview. Their approach, if not their language, is often consistent with the imaginative, humanistic direction urged in this book.

Also, in order to speed your involvement, I have not offered extensive examples of successful oral history. To have done so would have greatly lengthened the book, for good oral history is full of detail and cannot be succinctly quoted. Rather than lengthily quoting some of the best oral histories, I have briefly but critically discussed them in a way that, I hope, will encourage you to turn soon or someday to the books themselves. This approach offers you greater intellectual challenge and responsibility. And, after all, the reading of this book is meant less as a learning experience itself than as an introduction to another experience—the *activity* of oral history research. The most significant integration will be achieved not by this book but by you.

Oral history will obviously be most likely to be useful to you in recent and contemporary history courses. Your instructors in such courses will probably agree to oral history as part of your research efforts, provided that you can convince them that the oral research has historical significance. This requirement may seem a large obstacle, because of our almost automatic assumption that significant information can only be acquired from "important"—and therefore difficult to interview—people. Obviously, an ex-president or senator, famous philosopher, author, actor, military leader, industrialist, business person, or some other VIP can tell us things about important events, events of national significance. But is it possible to interview such people? Yes, it is, though it may require hard work, persistence, and luck. Peter Joseph, a Princeton undergraduate in the late 1960s and early 1970s, showed exemplary initiative in interviewing hundreds of people, many of them famous, for his senior thesis, which was later published under the title *Good Times: An Oral History of America in the 1960's*.[5] But most students will not interview nationally prominent figures, which is why Part Two of this book is meant to aid you in giving the interview significance by placing it in cultural and social context. Also, it is well to remember that "historical significance" is a relative term. Persons who are not nationally prominent may count for much on the regional, state, or local scene. Doctors, lawyers, judges, clergy, politicians, and newspaper editors may be excellent and important sources within a local context.

Furthermore, the best interviewee is quite likely to be someone who has never been interviewed before. Famous people are so experienced at separating public life from private that they may find it difficult to be not only honestly retrospective but also introspective in an interview. Tending to omit specific, personal details, they also leave out the "feel" for the facts. Jean Stein, in conducting interviews for *American Journey: The Times of Robert Kennedy*, found that "the freshest, most informative material seemed to come less from the pub-

5. Unfortunately, Joseph's book suffers from the same weakness as Terkel's *Hard Times*: no interest in written documents or in establishing significant historical contexts.

lic figures than from those for whom being interviewed must have been a novelty, the women particularly. . . ."[6] The wives had the vantage point of their famous husbands, but not being celebrities, they were not jaded interviewees.

It should also be possible to find ordinary people who have something to tell us about an important event. For example, in a course on the history of American labor you might decide that you want to write a paper on a strike that occurred in the last thirty or forty years. Many people involved in the strike, whether workers or managers, are likely to be still alive. Interviews with them could be an important supplement to information you would find in old newspapers, company and union records, and previously published studies. From interviews you might find out additional facts not only about what things happened but also about why they happened. The emotions that went into obstructing a public highway or hiring strikebreakers are the least likely things to be preserved in official records. Someone present at a union or company meeting is much more likely to be informative on emotions than a secretary's minutes. And you should consider the inner, human significance of the strike. How did it affect the people who lived through it? Did management harden or soften? Were workers more or less militant as a result of the strike? Were there any shifts in cultural values, say in the concept of the rights of private property?

But this last sort of research, on a cultural value, is the kind most likely to be resisted by your teacher, who may think that the question is vague and that you cannot make any significant generalizations on the basis of an interview or two. Actually, the representativeness of a small number of interviewees can be high, especially if they are articulate, intro-

6. P. x.

spective people.[7] If representativeness is a goal, try to balance your sample by interviewing, say, a worker and a manager. You should also try to explain that the interviews are to supplement traditional written sources by providing information in depth, information that gets its significance as much from its "thickness" as from its representativeness. None of these tactics availing, you have to decide whether or not to take the course, basing your decision, naturally, on all relevant factors—the quality of the course in other respects, degree requirements, and so on. Your teacher may also doubt that it is feasible or practical to attempt a specific research project, and it may be to your advantage to respect those doubts.

Although oral history usually involves interviewing older people, there is no reason why interviewees cannot be young. If you are writing a paper on some aspect of the Vietnam War, a thirty-year-old person might be a good source. For even more recent events, it is possible that a good interviewee might be in his teens or even younger, if he was in a time and place relevant to your topic.

No matter what topic you decide to work on, asking yourself some critical questions at the beginning can save wasted effort. Will interviewing be genuinely useful? If not, don't interview for the sake of interviewing. If you want the experience of doing oral history, find another topic where it will be useful. Consider practical problems. Will you have time to do the number of interviews you think are necessary? Two or three interviews are almost certainly the maximum you should plan for a term paper; you will find that preparing for, conducting, and using the results of just one interview can be very time-consuming. Also, will you have time and

7. Lewis A. Dexter, *Elite and Specialized Interviewing*, p. 8.

money enough to travel to the site of the interview? For many students, the ideal interviewee will be someone who lives near school or home.

But oral history research is not necessarily limited to American history courses. Travel overseas for a summer or an entire year is a reasonable hope for many students. If you do plan to visit another country, you may want to consider doing an oral history project there. But you should be aware that in many countries it is much harder than in the United States to get people to talk frankly to strangers.[8] Discuss the possible problems and complications in such a project with someone, perhaps a college faculty member, who has been to the country in question and knows its culture well. Despite the potential difficulties, oral history research may greatly enhance your understanding of another people. And the contact with local people it requires might be an excellent way to break through cultural and linguistic barriers, making your trip less lonely.

Finally, students who cannot undertake interviews for some reason—the resistance of a teacher, a topic so remote in time that potential interviewees are dead, lack of travel funds or time—may still be able to use oral history material. Many transcripts of interviews on file in oral history collections are available on microfilm or through interlibrary loan. Also, many history books are based in part on interviews. These documents can be useful, provided they are subjected to the same critical questions you should ask of oral documents you have gathered yourself. Therefore, the last chapter of this book discusses how to locate and use oral history documents collected by others.

8. See, for instance, Daniel Lerner, "Interviewing Frenchmen," pp. 187–94.

PART TWO

3

Personality

The number and complexity of the forces at work in human life make it impossible for us to think about them in any meaningful way unless we can divide them into a few general and therefore manageable categories. Given that we exist as individuals, social scientists have invented at least three different large categories for the human influences upon us:

"Society" refers to the sheer physical fact that we live among other people who have at least partly the power to permit us to do some things and prevent us from doing others.

"Culture" is the category for essentially intellectual influences—the ideas, knowledge, customs, values, and attitudes (either learned or invented)—that enable us to see some possible avenues of behavior and blind us to others.

"Personality," finally, is the individual response to cultural and social influences, the idiosyncratic interpretation of them by our unique selves, with the result that we prefer one course of behavior to another.

All three influences are interrelated to the extent of helping to determine one another, as well as our behavior. It is crucial not to lose sight of their complex interactions, but for the sake of discussion we will treat them, and the relation of oral history to them, in separate chapters. This chapter will be devoted to personality and the following two chapters, respectively, to culture and society.

One great virtue of oral history is its focus on the individual and consequently on personality. Sometimes culture and society are discussed at such a high level of abstraction that we forget that only through the behavior of individual personalities do the concepts of culture and society have meaning. Many historians argue that a focus on social change is what distinguishes history from "static" social sciences like anthropology. Yet "social change" is also an abstraction that has no meaning and cannot be explained without focusing on individual human behavior. For instance, social historians have generally been baffled by large-scale social change in the eighteenth and nineteenth centuries, and for explanation some have resorted to frankly idealistic concepts, like "modernization."[1] Such a concept will not be convincing or enlightening until it is shown how it helps us understand changes in behavior. That demonstration requires detailed accounts of how the concept is manifested in individual lives—an admittedly difficult goal for the bottom ranks of industrial society that interest many social historians. Yet one suspects that more could be done than is being done and that social scientists and social historians need not make the individual, in the critical phrase of one sociologist, "less than a phantom."[2]

In twentieth-century history it is still possible to speak with individuals who have experienced or are experiencing social

1. See, for instance, Richard D. Brown, *Modernization*, esp. pp. 19–21.

2. John Dollard, *Criteria for the Life History*, p. 16.

change. Therefore, there is no excuse for failing to recognize that individuals, who feel and think and act, are an important source for history. Robert Coles put the case eloquently in his *Children of Crisis*, writing about individual children in public schools where the color line was first broken in the South:

> I decided that there was every reason to study individuals facing desegregation in the South; in contrast, that is to desegregation as a "process" or "problem." . . . what of the individual people who have lived and do live in the midst of history . . . ? Ought we not learn how particular and various Southerners think and feel about the rather obvious troubles and even dangers they face—inadvertently, reluctantly, angrily, or because they feel the necessity? Black and white, old and young, rich and poor, people by the many hundred thousand stand by and in a number of ways react as laws and custom change. . . .
>
> How are we to know what those people truly feel—deep down?[3]

How, in short, are we to understand social change and social history unless we focus on the individual? For it is he or she who thinks and feels and may be able to reveal something of the propelling force that moves him or her and perhaps others. Oral history's focus on the individual therefore should enable it to make a significant contribution to social history.

The "life history" of either a famous or an ordinary individual, told in one or more interview sessions, is the most popular sort of oral history project and could make an excellent subject for a term paper. Yet there are some possibly large pitfalls in such a project that require care and effort to avoid. Within the confines of a term paper you will obviously not be able to tell the complete story of a person's life. This should not be too great a frustration if you recognize that no biography, even a book of hundreds of pages, ever presents

3. P. 18.

more than a small fraction of the experience in a normal life span of tens of thousands of days. But the danger is that the impossibility of completeness will tempt you to merely randomly select, for inclusion in your paper, the at least superficially interesting facts of the person's life. If your paper is merely a detailed list of unrelated events in a person's life, it will not be much above the level of gossip. And even if the person is a celebrity, your paper will have no legitimate claim on the attention of any reader who already has enough things to think about, things of probably greater personal interest to him than the subject of your paper.

On the other hand, your paper will have historical significance if the interviewee's life history is seen as a continuously related interaction of his personality, culture, and social situation. Your task, both in conducting the interview and in writing about it, is to find the key events in which the complex interactions of these forces can be seen. Only if the life history is seen to be all of a piece can it have any broad significance for other human beings who may share some of the interviewee's culture and social situation. But precisely because most of a person's cultural and social situations are to a degree shared by at least some other people, it is usually the individual personality that makes each account distinct. In order to relate the individual life story to the broader culture and society, it is crucial that the interviewer develop a sense of the interviewee's personality and the effect it has had upon his experiences.

To develop that "sense " of the personality, you need not be a Freudian psychoanalyst. The concern here is not with questions of personality formation that in the end may be unanswerable. It is possible that mastering psychoanalytic techniques would help us understand what Nate Shaw, of *All God's Dangers*, went through psychologically—what his inner experiences were like—and that would be an important contribution. But psychoanalysis still would not tell us why he responded to those experiences as he did. *Why* Nate rebelled against his oppressive father and became a heroic personality, while one of his brothers was permanently cowed, may always be a mystery, related perhaps to an unknowable quality in his soul.[4] What matters to the historian is that Nate *was* stubbornly heroic in facing down white landlords, sheriff's deputies, and finally, prison. If we do not recognize his heroism, we will underestimate the obstacles he and other black sharecroppers faced. The heroic dimension of his personality and the enormity of the cultural and social obstacles he overcame can be understood only together, in the context of his life history.

To achieve the understanding of personality required in oral history, then, you can begin by drawing on and continuing to develop social skills you have been using all your life. We all make judgments about the personalities of other people (which we are sometimes not wise enough to keep to ourselves). Even if we express those judgments in no more sophisticated a way than to say "I like him" or "I don't like him," they are still judgments of personality. That there is always room for improvement in our skill at making such judgments is evident from the common experience of having had our first impression of someone proved wrong when we have gotten to know him better. That experience should alert us to the need of getting to know the other person as well as

4. I first heard Robert Coles express this idea in a lecture at the Boston Public Library in the fall of 1977.

possible. Furthermore, detailed knowledge of a person and his life enables us to arrive at more complex judgments, to recognize that a person may have had experiences that explain qualities we don't like; for example, a morbid person, unpleasant to be with, may have seen much death. Or we may recognize that a person has admirable qualities even though we don't like him. A statement of this latter sort, though we seldom face the fact, may imply negative qualities in us, because we presumably should like the admirable. Or we may only be intelligently sorting out the good from the bad. But we can hardly grow in our knowledge of personality and skill in judging it unless we grow also in ourselves and our self-knowledge.

Learning about the interviewee's personality is important even if you are using oral history in a research project more traditional than a life history. In a more traditional project, the interviewee himself may not be the main focus of attention. Perhaps he is a witness to another person's life or a participant in some event that is the subject of your research. Yet you still need to make a decision about his reliability as a witness. Does he seem honest, and beyond that, does he seem able and willing to deal objectively with the past? Does he have a vested interest—his own reputation to protect, for instance—that might stand in the way of an accurate account, and does he seem consciously to attempt to overcome that interest as he remembers the past? Answers to these questions must be based partly on your impression of him and his behavior during the interview. Therefore, even in relating oral history to a fairly traditional research project, it may be necessary to spend part of your time and energy learning about the interviewee. Of course, you will inevitably form some impression of anyone with whom you talk for an hour or more. But in addition to the main topic, you may also want to discuss briefly some other aspects of the interviewee's life. Childhood and work are good focal points for this kind of quick investigation, as they will reveal something of his cultural training and social situation—factors against which any intelligent judgment of personality must be made.

If you undertake a life history, it is crucial to discuss the interviewee's early family life. The family is the child's first society, and through its demands he acquires his earliest cultural training. In childhood experiences it is often possible to see both the development of personality and the pattern of its interaction with culture and society. For example, the development of an adult's pattern of response to authority—teachers, bosses, police, and so on—might be seen in his early relations with his parents. To state this fact is not to take a deterministic view of personality but only to recognize that the personal and cultural equipment with which an individual responds to a new experience has been forged in past experiences. The individual is free to use that equipment in new and possibly liberating ways. But if history in general and life history in particular have any meaning and merit study, it can only be because of underlying continuities between present actions and past experiences.

The life history must also be viewed against the social situation, both in childhood and adulthood. Into what kind of family, neighborhood, and economic class was the person born? What schools, friends, and recreation were available to him? Did he marry and have children? Did he begin to work during a time of prosperity or depression? What kind of work did he find, and how has it affected other parts of his life? What kind of neighborhood does he live in now, and does he earn enough money for his needs? And though these questions are principally about the individual's social situation, cultural and personal factors will have helped determine many of the answers—the amount of money, for instance, that he "needs." Again, then, it is necessary to see the life history as a whole, across time, and in the context of culture and society.

4
Culture

Oral history, we have said, can deal with the experiences not only of the famous but also of ordinary people whose lives may have intersected with some historic event. Such people often do not leave many written documents except of the kind that can be dealt with statistically—census records, deeds, birth and death certificates, and the like. Thus, it may be only through talking with them that we can learn the inner facts of their lives—their emotions, ideas, attitudes, and feelings. Inner facts, revealed in the spoken words of individuals, are crucial to an understanding of the full human and historical significance of an event. After all, "statistics don't bleed," as Robert Jay Lifton noted in his book *Death in Life*, a psychological oral history of the survivors of the atomic bombing of Hiroshima. Estimates of how many died in the explosion range from sixty-three to four hundred thousand, but such figures do not convey either the horror or the meaning found in the spoken memories of a single survivor:

The appearance of people was . . . well, they all had skin blackened by burns. . . . They had no hair because their hair was burned, and at a glance you couldn't tell whether you were looking at them from in front or in back. . . . They held their arms bent [forward] like

> this [he proceeded to demonstrate their position] . . . and their skin—not only on their hands, but on their faces and bodies too—hung down. . . . If there had been only one or two such people . . . perhaps I would not have had such a strong impression. But wherever I walked I met these people. . . . Many of them died along the road—I can still picture them in my mind—like walking ghosts. . . . They didn't look like people of this world.[1]

This sense of having been to another world, a world of death in life, and the consequent dangers of alienation and psychic closing off from other people threatens, according to Lifton, not only the survivors of the original blast but all of us in the nuclear age. What has happened before can happen again. Knowing that an entire city has been destroyed by one bomb makes the same fate seem a more real danger for us. This inner fact, this change in human consciousness, may be of great historical significance, and we can learn that fact, not through statistics, but through the words of the survivors.

Ordinary people who have never been subjected to an atomic explosion may also tell us much about the inner facts of history. To say that people are ordinary should not imply that they are standardized, interchangeable parts of the social machine. It suggests only that, unlike celebrities, they are not very visible as individuals. Historians, therefore, tend to treat such people as members of groups. For instance, the civil rights movement of the 1950s and 1960s depended heavily on the mass support of ordinary blacks. Therefore, a historian wishing to explain the civil rights movement might say that blacks as a group were increasingly militant. A survey questionnaire given to large numbers of blacks, asking for multiple choice answers, such as "yes," "no," or "maybe," might

1. P. 27.

prove the assertion correct. Yet how much is explained by the statement that blacks were increasingly militant? Might we not want to know *why* they were increasingly militant? And why at that time rather than twenty years earlier or later? It may not be possible to answer such questions with certitude, but we will surely come much closer if, rather than soliciting short answers from a large sampling, we listen at length to individuals, as Robert Hamburger did in his powerful, disturbing book *Our Portion of Hell*, an oral history of the struggle for civil rights in Fayette County, Tennessee.

It is interesting to compare Hamburger's work to Howell Raines's book *My Soul Is Rested: Movement Days in the Deep South Remembered*. Raines's work has no real geographical focus (other than the South), and his interviews of mostly famous civil rights leaders, though arranged in coherent groupings, do not shed much light on one another. The result is that, as with Terkel's book on the depression, we are glad to read the detailed accounts of some interesting people, but we gain little historical insight beyond the popular images of marches and sit-ins we already possessed. Raines's work will not achieve its greatest, and even then fairly limited, usefulness till a historian places it in the context of thousands of other equally important documents available on the civil rights movement.

Hamburger, on the other hand, reveals the deep local roots of discontent that were the real springs of action in Fayette County. At the same time, he brings the headline stories of the 1960s into sharp focus by showing how Civil Rights Acts, Lyndon Johnson's War on Poverty, and Richard Nixon's Southern Strategy impinged on the lives of local people. All this is achieved by a sort of cinematic cutting and splicing of individual accounts, which, almost ironically, gives not the "kaleidoscopic" effect some compilers of oral history say they strive for[2] but rather the traditional, logical order of narrative history. Furthermore, Hamburger's is no satisfied book of victors looking proudly back on past glories. His interviewees, perhaps partly because they are still embattled, convincingly recall the feeling of past struggles. His book has an inwardness that, not despite but because of its detailed local context, makes it an important historical account of the mass civil rights movement.

Hamburger's success at giving meaning to individual accounts by placing them in a significant context indicates how historians can best use the technique of the interview, which is usually used *only* to study individual facts, ideas, and personalities. Journalists, lawyers, doctors, teachers, and prospective employers all engage often in interviewing, but with the purpose of finding out about one particular person or thing. Some critics might therefore dispute the idea that when we interview an individual we learn about anything more than that particular person. How can we generalize about history by interviewing ordinary individuals who may not even seem to be involved in history as we encounter it in textbooks focused on "great" events and "great" people? The answer must lie in relating their experiences to those of other people in the cultural and social groups to which they belong.

Here the anthropological concept of culture is especially useful. In *The Cultural Experience*, a book designed to introduce anthropology students to field work, James Spradley

2. Peter Joseph, *Good Times*, p. vii. Michael Lesy, though not an oral historian, has used a cinematic analogy to justify his innovative compilations. A discussion of Lesy's work and its significance for oral history may be found below in chapter 7, "Preparing for the Interview."

and David McCurty define culture as "knowledge which people use to generate and interpret social behavior."[3] Culture, in other words, is all of our ideas that cause us to behave as we do and to respond to others' behavior as we do. We are taught many of these ideas by other members of groups to which we belong, groups as small as families and as large as nations. Learning table manners from one's parents or studying computers in college are both examples of cultural training. But the important point here is that much of our culture is determined by the particular society or group into which we are born. Being taught to use a fork rather than chop sticks is, at least initially, not a matter of choice but of fate. As we grow older, culture tends somewhat less to be formally taught to us, but we continue to acquire or perhaps invent new concepts as a result of immediate experience. Here, too, the experience may be shared with other people in a group determined by such factors as class, race, religion, sex, occupation, geographical proximity, and so on. Examples of shared group experiences could include going to college, fighting in a war, or working in a factory as opposed to an office. Culture, whether taught or acquired through experience, is usually shared by groups of people. Yet because culture is ideational—that is, composed of ideas and knowledge—individuals are the only possible sources for it. Culture is located, or, as anthropologists say, "carried," in the head, and only individuals have heads. To find out about the cultural or inner meaning of history we must study individual documents—letters, pictures, or oral history interviews.

Of course, individuals may be studied as members of a large group, as is often done in the survey questionnaires

3. P. 8.

with standardized answers used by many sociologists and pollsters. Survey questionnaires have advantages: not only can they be administered to large numbers of people but also, through sampling and statistical techniques, they can tell us about the ideas of still larger groups. But the statistical procedures involved require that the possible answers be the same for every respondent. Sometimes sophisticated attempts are made to word a large number of questions in such a way that one answer can be checked against another. But that process improves only the accuracy, not the richness, of the information. As long as the answers are standardized, the information obtained must be relatively "thin" and lacking in detail.

The thinness of standardized answers is illustrated by an experience of mine from the 1960s, when I was helping to distribute a multiple choice questionnaire on racial attitudes in a small Ohio town. Encountering a blind old white man who obviously could not fill out the questionnaire, I offered to read the questions aloud and fill in his answers for him. In response to "How do you feel about the Ku Klux Klan?" the old man reddened and said that he hated the Klan. So I checked "disapprove." But he went on, saying that when he had been a farmer forty years earlier, his best milk cow had been shot and killed during a rally of Klansmen in one of his neighbor's fields. He had hated the Klan ever since. Abandoning the questionnaire, I asked what he thought of the Klan's racial attitude. Race had not been a large issue, he answered, adding that one of the Klan's "problems" had been that there were few blacks and not even many Catholics, not to mention Jews, in rural Ohio. The local Klansmen had been forced to spend their energy running prostitutes out of town and beating up unfaithful husbands. Although further conversation proved the old man a racial bigot, his stance could not be revealed by a question which mistakenly assumed that race rather than cows would be the basis of his attitude toward the Klan.

This discrepancy did not necessarily invalidate the questionnaire, because numerous other questions might have gotten at the old man's racial attitudes and made the Klan question statistically insignificant. But the incident does show that if we want to understand not only what someone thinks but *why* he thinks it, we would do well to ask him to answer in his own words rather than ours. Questionnaires with standardized answers are good as far as they go, but they do not go very far in the direction of reasons and motives. That sort of information is best obtained in detailed, "open-ended" interviews, where the respondent is free to answer at length and in his own words. Although it is not possible to interview as many people in this way as with a standardized questionnaire, there is the offsetting advantage that the information obtained in open-ended interviews is much more detailed.

Culture, being knowledge, ideas, attitudes, and values, is complex, and the study of culture therefore requires careful, detailed description, "thick description," as one anthropologist has put it.[4] The virtue of the open-ended interview in oral history is precisely the kind of detail it provides, especially on reasons and motives. Though it is more difficult to generalize from such individualized information, its detail, its "thickness," is more likely to reveal inner, cultural meaning. Therefore, even in political science and sociology, open-ended interviewing is an important research technique. In history, where the factors of lapsed time and memory create

4. Clifford Geertz, *The Interpretation of Cultures*, p. 6.

complications, detail and thickness are of the utmost importance. If the old man's blindness had not forced me to listen to his long-winded but detailed answers, I would have missed an important insight into the appeal and role of the Ku Klux Klan in local history. Cultural history, in the sense of the ideas and values of ordinary people, has scarcely begun to be written, and oral history, with its open-ended interviews, can make an important contribution to it.

For your term paper you might choose a topic in cultural history, a topic about change and/or continuity in the thought and ideas of people as revealed in some aspect of their customs and habits, ranging from creating works of art to playing street games. Ethnic groups make excellent sources for such studies because of the drastic changes and adjustments they have often made in accommodating themselves to American society. But people's cultures change not only as they move from place to place but also as their society moves through time. Many people today have practices in dress, work, and sexual relationships different from those of their parents or even themselves only a few years ago. These changes are as worthy of historical study as many others, and because of the personal nature of the required information, oral history should be an especially useful research technique for making such studies.

If you do study a problem in cultural history, be sure to keep the project manageable. Focus on one custom or habit, as is done, for instance, in the accounts of hog dressing, snake lore, moonshining, and other topics treated in the *Foxfire* books. These well-known collections of mountain folklore are based on interviews conducted by high school students in Rabun Gap, Georgia. Probably, most readers of *this* book will not be ideally situated to collect mountain folklore, but the *Foxfire* students' attention to detail on single topics is a model of humanistic and apparently personally satisfying research. There will be many individual topics in your local culture that you can begin to study in the same way: customs and habits of work, recreation, religious faith, and daily living.

But college students in history courses should have a more ambitious goal than the *Foxfire* students' objective of merely collecting information on customs, folklore, and habits. Whatever cultural item you study should be related to the broader culture and society. One of the most successful papers in a course on the depression I taught at Harvard dealt with the establishment of dog-racing tracks in Massachusetts. The student used interviews of people who attended the races not only to understand the cultural significance of the event but also to gain insight into Massachusetts politics as they were reflected in the issue of licensing gambling on dog races.

Whatever the cultural item you choose, you can heighten the historical significance of your study by asking critical questions about the personal and social function of the item. Does the belief or practice have special significance for individuals, say by giving meaning and diffusing sorrow, as funeral rites sometimes do? Has the belief or practice changed as a response to people's social experience—emigration, technological change, economic shifts, and so on? And culture should not be viewed as a merely passive register of social forces. Culture may also actively help determine people's social experience. An ethnic or some other social group, for instance, may have cultural values that encourage its members to look for one sort of work and avoid another even at economic cost.

Taking an active view of culture is a difficult intellectual challenge and one that is not always well met by historians, who usually find it easier to think of the social situation, which is more visible and quantifiable. But historians are surely correct in insisting upon the necessity of relating culture to the society in which it is used. Similarly, anthropologists are never satisfied merely to listen to people whose spoken cultural ideals are often belied by their social actions. For example, many Americans pay lip service to high ideals in church and temple, but as social critics often remind us, their habits at work and play show that there is also a very materialistic aspect to their values. Therefore, anthropologists try to learn the meaning and significance of culture as it is manifested in social *behavior*. A good anthropologist is not only a good listener but also a good observer. Obviously, you as an oral historian cannot directly observe your interviewee's past actions. Yet even when you are primarily interested in ideas and emotions, they should always be discussed in relation to behavior. Finding out what the interviewee's ideas led him to do is one good test of the significance of the ideas themselves. You can learn about his past behavior, not only by asking him about it, but sometimes also from written documents. Acquiring as much detailed, factual information as possible about the interviewee's behavior is essential to understanding its cultural implications.

But even then you cannot make intelligent deductions about the cultural meaning of his behavior unless you are familiar with the outer, social context that also constrained his actions. Therefore, we must now consider the use of oral documents in studying the history of society.

5
Society

We use our culture, our ideas and knowledge, to understand and interpret the world around us and thus to determine what action or behavior is right for us. Yet culture is far from being the only cause of our actions. Geography and climate, for instance, also limit the range of possible behavior open to us. Climate rather than culture makes it impossible for Eskimos to go naked and for Polynesians to dress in furs. Yet culture does help determine how Polynesians choose to dress from among the countless possibilities available in their region and climate. After nonhuman factors such as climate and geography, and in addition to factors like culture and personality, some of the most powerful determinants of the possible behavior open to *us* are *other* people around us, their interrelationships, and their behavior.

"Society" is the simplest name for this whole human world we live in. Understanding, interpreting, and changing society is one of the most important purposes of culture. And culture in turn is partly shaped and determined by society. The relationship between "society" and "culture," then, is so close and complex that, understandably, the two words are sometimes used almost interchangeably, as if they meant about the same thing. But they mean very different things, and the distinction ought to be kept clear. A person's culture, being ideas, knowledge, attitudes, and values, is located or carried in his head, whereas his society, being other people, is outside him. Culture, says the anthropologist Sidney Mintz, "is *used*." Culture is "a kind of resource" and society is the "arena" in which that resource is used.[1] If culture is to be studied by observing behavior, it is necessary to distinguish cultural from social causes of behavior. Social causes are those due to the shape and structure of the social "arena" in which culture is used. To study culture we must also study society.

Societies are often so complex and enormous that oral history, based on the perceptions and accounts of individuals, may seem too limited a tool for researching them. In studying a society it is often necessary to sacrifice "thickness," or detail, in order to achieve any general grasp of the subject at all; we must lose sight of individual trees if we back up far enough to see the forest. Statistics based on standardized questionnaires and on research in census and other written records are far more likely to give us an overall view of the social "arena" than the spoken memories of a few individuals. Lamentably, the charts, graphs, and tables in which the statistics are presented lack human detail, but at least we get a general picture, however sketchy and thin.

Yet precisely because of that thinness, oral history and other qualitative sources have an important role to play in social history, for they colorfully and vividly fill in at least small corners of our otherwise sketchy picture of society, relating it to individual human lives. We will not genuinely

1. Mintz, Foreword to *Afro-American Anthropology*, p. 10.

understand social history if we lose sight of the fact that it has no existence apart from the people who, together, are the society. It is easy to forget that people create social as well as all other kinds of history. Some people may feel and in fact be powerless in the face of social change, but even this powerlessness can be understood only by studying the relationship between society and the individual. Qualitative sources serve this crucial purpose of bringing social history to life, revealing its significance and meaning for individual human beings and thus giving *it* meaning. For instance, the statistic that the unemployment rate reached 20 percent during the depression of the 1930s also shows that four out of five people still had jobs—a fact that might make the depression seem a less crucial national experience than it was. Only through such individual, qualitative sources as letters, diaries, novels, or oral histories can we get at the depth of suffering experienced by an unprecedentedly large number of Americans. The reduced expectations and heightened fear of countless others and thus the meaning of the depression itself can be obtained only through qualitative sources. Yet it is true, too, that severe as the depression was, qualitative sources taken alone might lead us to overestimate its severity. In studying a society as large as the United States, there is no discounting the absolute necessity for statistical measurement.

Combining quantitative and qualitative sources can also be a fruitful approach to studying smaller societies. Many social historians do study small communities, and if the study is set in the recent past, oral history can make a significant contribution to it. Ronald Blythe's *Akenfield: Portrait of an English Village* is almost certainly the finest oral history ever published. Yet the secret of the book's success lies not only in the spoken words of the villagers, but also in Blythe's sensitive, beautifully written introductions to the narratives. There he unobtrusively uses statistics to set the narratives in a context of regional and national social history. Or to put it more accurately, the narratives serve mainly to illuminate Blythe's shorter but essential social history of the English countryside. His brief but wonderfully effective introductions also help create personalities for the speakers and relate their accounts to their occupations and to experiences not in the narratives. Social historians, we must hope, will increasingly merge quantitative and qualitative sources, and those who can would do well to model their writing on Blythe's.

Even in studying the history of a family (the smallest social unit there is), the larger society around it must be taken into account. Otherwise, we lose one of the main advantages of focusing on so small a social group—the opportunity to see how complex the interaction is between cultural and social forces. There has been much talk in the last decade, for instance, of a "culture of poverty," as if poverty and its accompanying sadness were somehow only a problem of the mental outlook of the poor. Doubtless there is something in this concept, as is illustrated by Dorothy Gallagher's fine family and oral history *Hannah's Daughters*, dealing with a line of mothers and daughters reaching back six generations and nearly a hundred years. In the first four generations, each woman married a man who failed to support her, and each woman was eventually divorced. This is an impressive statistic, given the relative infrequency of divorce in the latter part of the nineteenth and early part of the twentieth centuries. And the women themselves, in the interviews, attributed their problems to their having poor examples of family life in childhood—which supports the concept of a "culture of poverty." Yet the women's narratives also show that they and their husbands experienced staggering economic problems related mainly to their vulnerable social position as workers and field hands, which had little to do with their culture or mental outlook. Many "successful" marriages, composed of people with secure, prosperous childhoods, might have fared no better if they had been tested by economic and social stresses so severe. If poverty were only a cultural problem, it would be easy for more comfortable people to urge its eradication through education and enlightenment. But, in fact, it is a social problem as well—which means that the opportunities of some people are purchased at the expense of others. Recognizing that fact and deciding what to do about it are severe moral issues that the American middle and upper classes have never successfully faced.

We are all far more deeply involved in and affected by social and therefore political history than we usually realize. In our increasingly complex and centralized society, our individual lives are likely to be affected by "great" but seemingly remote historical issues. The energy crisis, the inflated cost of health care, the aging of our population, devaluations of the dollar, and so on affect us now and will probably lead to political decisions in the near future that will have a powerful impact on the course of all our lives. Yet many of us feel detached from such decisions, not only because we have little to do with making them, but also because we seem mistakenly to think that they will have little effect on us. Many of us now, despite the immediacy of television, seem to feel the way one of Hannah's daughters says she felt during the Second World War: "in those days things didn't seem so close to you. We'd see things in newsreels, but that was maybe a week after they happened."[2] But as Dorothy Gallagher shows

2. Dorothy Gallagher, *Hannah's Daughters*, p. 213.

in her excellent introductory passages and as the narratives themselves attest, the lives of these women were greatly affected by wars, depressions, and other historical events of their times. So were the lives of our parents and ancestors. One of the virtues of studying the involvement of our own families in history is that the process should help awaken us to our own inescapable involvement.

Seeing that involvement, however, is not always easy. If you interview your parents or grandparents, do not expect that they, any more than Hannah's daughters, will automatically be eloquent witnesses to the importance for individual human experience of wars, depressions, and other "historical" events. They may even feel that theirs are commonplace stories in relation to *history*. For them, the central and dramatic events of their lives may have been going to school, finding or losing a job, moving from one place to another, getting married, and having children. One suspects, in fact, that many families almost consciously cultivate the feeling of being securely tucked away in routine jobs and homes and schools, safe from the vicissitudes of history. It is therefore up to you as a historian to provide the insight and imagination, as well as the background research, that link individual life histories to social history. If a factory closed and left your grandfather unemployed, you may have to do background research in written materials to show the link between that event and the national economic depression of the 1930s. If your Jewish grandmother herself makes the connection between life history and social history by saying that she fled religious persecution in Europe, it is still up to you to get the details, both from her and from written sources, that will make "persecution" more than an impersonal abstraction. *How* did persecution endanger your grandmother—economically, socially, mortally? Was her sole motive social injustice in the old country, or was she partly attracted to America by a positive vision of it? Detail is essential in understanding the complex relationship between the individual and the culture and society around him.

Among students, research projects on the history of their own families are growing in popularity, and justifiably so. Students should have a chance to attain the personal awareness of the connections between social history and their own heritage that such projects can provide. There is, however, no reason that you could not focus on another family, instead of your own, except that finding another family willing to deal with you as cooperatively and frankly as your own might prove difficult. Still, we should not get the idea that "family history" means studying only our own families. Studying others more distant from ourselves may present a greater challenge and be even more educational. And there are other possible projects, involving larger social groups than the family, which you might want to undertake. The entire history of a neighborhood or community will probably not be manageable, but you could focus on a single event—such as a strike, the integration of a school, the closing of a factory, or a natural disaster—and the effect of the event on the community. And oral history interviews with people involved in the event might contribute significantly to your project. But many students will want to work on the family, which, as the smallest social unit, offers a good focus for a coherent and manageable term project.

The next part of this book will be devoted to interviewing techniques in general, but here it may be well to suggest a general strategy for family history interviews. Usually, the interview should be an attempt to relate family history to the larger culture and society around it, and a good way of getting at these connections may be to move from the family's *internal* to its *external* experience. Examples of questions relating to the family's internal experience would be how and where the family lived, what social activities went on inside the family, and who exercised authority and control within the family. Under these broad categories there are many interesting questions; did relatives and married sons or daughters live in the house; who slept where; was there indoor plumbing; were there servants or boarders; how were holidays spent; what happened at weddings and funerals; how were important questions, such as whether to move to a new place, decided; who disciplined the children and how; what sorts of conflicts occurred between family members; when did sons and daughters leave home; and who cared for the old and the sick? External experience would involve such matters as who worked where; how much they were paid; whether they were satisfied with their work; what social activities, such as bars, clubs, and churches, were available outside the family to men and to women; what boys and girls did together and how courtship was conducted; whether family members served in the military; whether there were experiences of immigration or uprooting moves, and the reasons for them; whether there was involvement in wars, depressions, or other "historic" events; and what effects technological change and mass media had on the family, especially between generations. But, as will be emphasized again, the purpose of such guidelines is to help you get as much useful information in as many areas as possible. Every interview is a unique human experience, and guidelines that work with one interviewee may stifle another. In the latter case it is not the interviewee but the guidelines that should be abandoned.

PART THREE

6

Arranging the Interview

Whomever you want to interview, attempt to contact him or her at the beginning of the term. Advance planning is important for simple, practical reasons. If the potential interviewee is a busy person, his calendar will be likely to be filled up if you do not put in your request early. Everyone, busy or not, finds it easier to promise to do something weeks or months from now than tomorrow. And if it is not possible to interview the desired person, you need to learn that fact quickly, before you have invested much time in a project you may not be able to complete. All these thoughts on the advantages of starting early apply to you even if you live next door to the interviewee or think you have a special connection. One student I know wanted to interview a famous writer who was going to lecture on campus near the end of the semester, but she would not bother to contact the writer in advance. She counted on a personal introduction from her best friend, the student who was in charge of the lecture series. As a result, she was just one of dozens of people the writer met in a short, hectic visit, and there was no time for an interview.

In addition to starting early, consideration for the interviewee is the other major rule followed by those successful in getting and conducting oral history interviews. Oral history methods should not be modeled on the popular image of the brash, aggressive reporter (sometimes confirmed by television journalists) who tramples into disaster-stricken lives in order to get a sensational story. Again I can cite the example of a student, a journalism major, who tried to get an oral history interview with a busy, famous person by writing an initial letter that was, in his words, "as outrageous as possible." Not surprisingly, the student did not get an answer, not to mention an interview. Whether the rights of a free press and the need of an informed public justify such journalists in all their methods, their ruder tactics will seldom work with potential oral history interviewees who seldom feel the same compelling pressure to talk about the past which those caught up in contemporary events often feel about the present. Furthermore, the best, most searching, and most interesting interviews, whether conducted by reporters or by historians, are never unnecessarily antagonistic but involve, as far as possible, a cooperative exploration of the issue at hand. Sometimes intellectual honesty requires questions that provoke hostile feelings, but the hostility will usually get in the way of thought. Antagonism should be minimized whenever possible, for both practical and intellectual reasons, and it is certainly foolish to arouse it in the process merely of arranging the interview. An energetic, active approach to obtaining the interview need not conflict with basic rules of courtesy and consideration.

A U.S. senator would probably be a quite difficult person with whom to get an interview, so let us imagine a case where a student wishes to do so. Amy Schwartz—from Chicago, interested and active in local politics there, and taking a course in recent political history—wants to write a term paper on Richard Daley's early political career in order better to understand the forces that made him mayor of the city. She decides that it would be useful to interview one of Daley's aides from that period, a man named, say, Thomas Shannon. If Mr. Shannon had retired in order to devote himself to a hobby, Amy might have found it fairly easy to get the interview. But, alas, he is now the senior senator from Illinois. Amy is somewhat discouraged at the prospect of trying to get an interview with such a busy and important person. But she reflects that she is one of his constituents and it is in his interest to do what he conveniently can for her. And she is interested in politics, an interest that the senator obviously shares.

These factors, however, will be more likely to do her some good if she has some special connection to the senator. Because she has been active in Chicago politics, even if only at the precinct level, she probably knows someone with some political influence who could call the senator or drop him a note saying that she is a worthy person and urging that he give her the interview. If so, the temptation will be great for Amy to rely solely on that person to arrange the interview, but that would be a serious mistake. She should view whatever support she can get as *only* support, and she herself should request the interview from the senator. By doing so she will both give tangible evidence of her genuine interest and also keep control of the matter in her own hands, which will make it easier to settle on details of place and time. Even if a third person were willing and responsible enough to make arrangements for Amy, letting him do so might invite unnecessary confusion. But she should definitely ask the third person for all the support he is willing to give.

If Amy does not have a special connection to the senator, there are other possible ways of strengthening her request. Does she work on the school paper, or can she at least get it to commission an article on Daley and the senator in the 1950s? If so, she could introduce herself as a reporter, whom politicians are usually glad to see. Still another possibility would be to find out if there is an oral history project that would like to obtain an interview of the senator and would be willing to designate Amy an "official interviewer." In general, whatever she can do to make herself a representative of an institution will increase her chances of getting the interview. But even if she cannot make any special connections, hard work, persistence, and a little luck may suffice.

Amy has telephoned James Dunn, a state legislator from Chicago for whom she campaigned and who has now promised to write to the senator in her behalf. So she decides to try to arrange an interview in Chicago in December, when she and perhaps the senator will be home on vacation. But right now it is September and Congress is in session. Presumably, the senator is in Washington. Obtaining his address there from the *U.S. Government Manual* (with the help of a reference librarian at the University of Illinois, where she is a student) Amy writes to him as follows:

333 Noble Hall
University of Illinois
Urbana, Ill. 61801
12 September 1979

Hon. Thomas Shannon
Room 138
Russell Office Building
Delaware and
Constitution Avenues
Washington, D.C. 20510

Dear Mr. Senator:

I am writing at the suggestion of Representative James Dunn to inquire if it would be possible for you to meet with me for an hour in Chicago this coming December in order to discuss Mayor Richard Daley's service as clerk of Cook County from 1950 to 1955. I am studying the mayor's early political career in order better to understand the personal qualities and historical forces that carried him to the top of Chicago politics. I am contacting you because I understand that you worked closely with him when he was county clerk. Though there are many printed sources—such as newspaper accounts— available for my study, they usually lack personal insight and do not emphasize the mayor's perspective. The recollections of the mayor's close associates are therefore an important historical source that, I believe, should be recorded, and I would bring along a tape recorder for that purpose.

In order to assure you that your time would not be misspent, I will add that I am a serious researcher and well acquainted with the political history of Chicago. During the next few months I will be learning much about the mayor's early political career from written records. I hope that our meeting would be an unusual and interesting opportunity for you to recall the past and to tell me about it in detail.

I am collecting this material for a paper I am writing in a course in recent American history. If any further use of the material (such as deposit in a library) becomes possible, you would be able to review the tape and transcript and have final decision over their use.

I will be home in Chicago this winter from 18 December to 3 January and would be happy to meet you at any time and place convenient to you in that period. If you will not be in Chicago then, perhaps the interview could be at another time or place. I look forward to the possibility of meeting you.

Sincerely yours,
Amy Schwartz

Note that Amy's letter is fairly brief, easy to read, and begins directly with her request and a clear statement of how much time she will need. It is usually a mistake to ask for more than an hour, even if you want more. You don't want to discourage the interviewee or, if he turns out to be tediously talkative, promise him too much listening. Once the interviewee's interest is engaged it may be possible to get him to give you more time. Notice also that Amy simply states that the interview will be tape recorded. Asking permission to tape is usually a mistake because it raises the possibility of a negative answer. Most people who agree to an interview will not mind having it taped. If the senator has an objection, he can raise it without Amy's help.

The letter's second paragraph assures the senator that he will have an interested, well-informed listener but ends by stressing that he will have a teaching role in the interview. Any anthropologist who has studied a jungle tribe will tell you that people talk more readily to an outsider if they believe that they are teaching him. Talking about oneself is a great pleasure, but one against which people often have social inhibitions. If it is justified by a didactic purpose, the inhibitions are usually easily overcome. The pleasure of teaching, of believing that one's own experiences and ideas have meaning for others, is a principal reason for most people's enjoyment of being interviewed. Being young and therefore teachable can be an advantage in getting an interview, and you, like Amy, may openly indicate that you are a student. You should, however, stress that you are serious and well prepared, which is unfortunately often not true of interviewers, whether students or not. (The next chapter discusses preparation.)

Amy's third paragraph explains the purpose of the research and assures the senator that his right to privacy will be respected, that nothing he says will be available to the public unless he chooses to make it available. This guarantee is important to public figures whose words might be scrutinized in the press, and it is equally important to private citizens whose words should not be made public unless they choose to make them so. The guarantee of privacy may help persuade the potential interviewee not only to grant the interview but also to speak frankly during it.

The final paragraph suggests a broad period of time for the interview. Because Amy is asking the senator to do her a favor, she owes it to him to make it as convenient as she can. But she also does herself a favor by leaving open the possibility of meeting somewhere other than Chicago or during another period of time. She does not want to make it easy for the senator to say no just because he is planning a Florida vacation. Perhaps she could and would like to go to Florida, too. Or, more likely, perhaps she can meet the senator in Chicago during Thanksgiving vacation.

If the senator does not answer Amy's letter, she may want to try again. Her first letter may have gone astray, or perhaps, though it is unlikely, he is discourteous enough not to answer. In either case, it might be profitable to write again, explaining the contents of the first letter in case it has gone undelivered or been forgotten. Once more, the emphasis should be on courtesy. Rather than accusing the senator of not answering,

Amy should imply that he may not have received her first letter. She might also offer to telephone on a specific date in order to save him the trouble of writing. Even if he intends to say no, an imminent phone call may at least provoke a written response. Better yet, her persistence may convince him that she is serious and make him decide to give her the interview. If he still does not answer, she may or may not decide to invest in the phone call. Perhaps she will get no farther than the office switchboard. But in case she does reach him, she should be prepared to state her request briefly and clearly.

Assuming that Amy does get the interview, she should make sure that the exact place and time are clear. Sometimes the interviewee will be vague on this question, even while agreeing to the interview. If so, she should settle the matter with another letter, perhaps suggesting a choice of times and places and enclosing a postcard for the senator's convenience in replying. Although she has left the interview site up to him in her first letter, she should probably try to avoid his office because of potential distractions there—pressing decisions, telephone calls, and other interruptions. The interviewee's home is usually a good place, though "neutral ground," some interviewers report, is even better.[1] At whatever point in the correspondence the place and time are settled, Amy should reply once more, agreeing to the specific arrangements so that the senator is left in no doubt.

The same rules of consideration and thoughtfulness apply also to less well-known persons, but methods of finding and approaching them differ from those for the famous.

1. Richard Sennett and Jonathan Cobb, *The Hidden Injuries of Class*, p. 41.

Suppose that in an American history course you become interested in the shift in the 1930s from private charity and volunteer efforts to government relief run by professional social workers. For your term paper you might decide to study that transition on the local level in your home town. It is quite possible that there will be someone still living there who was a fairly young social worker during the thirties. But finding that person will require a little more imagination and work than was needed for Amy to get Senator Shannon's address from a reference librarian. You will have to make some inquiries, beginning probably with friends and relatives, if they are long-time residents of the town. Social work agencies in the area will be another starting point and clergymen yet another. And if you succeed in locating the right person, you will want to stress whatever local contacts exist between you and him or her, making your request seem as much like that of a neighbor as possible.

If you are attempting one of the projects suggested in Part Two, such as a family history or the life history of an individual, the interviewee may be a friend or relative. Perhaps you can simply telephone or make your request in person, but you should still do so as soon as possible. If you do write, it would obviously be wrong to do so in the formal tone of Amy's letter to the senator.

There are still other potential sources for whom any letter at all might be too formal a means of contact. Someone who is poorly educated or who does not read English might only be frightened by a letter and should probably be approached personally. Sociologists, who have the most experience of studying such people in American society, usually recommend asking an intermediary, someone whom both you and the potential interviewee trust, to introduce you. It is sometimes possible, however, to get along without an intermediary. The illiterate Nate Shaw immediately took to and told the story of his life to Theodore Rosengarten, who went uninvited to Shaw's Alabama cabin. The result was *All God's Dangers*, an excellent as well as a best-selling book. (Luckily for Rosengarten, Shaw identified him with the young white radicals who had befriended him in the thirties, since Rosengarten looked a lot like them.) William Whyte, a very young sociologist at the time he researched *Street Corner Society* in the 1930s, was not so lucky. He was offered a barroom beating when he tried to join a party of two women and a man he did not know. He was able courteously to decline the offer, but it was a year and a half before Whyte met "Doc," the intermediary without whom he could not have written his book. So if you do not already know a possible intermediary, you should probably not attempt, in a term project, to interview people with a great deal less money and a different social status than you.

Working people, minority groups, and the poor often resent, and often rightfully so, the fact that they are forever studied by students and social scientists. The poor are aware of the implication in many studies that they are a social problem. It would be fair for them to ask if the selfishness of the middle and upper classes is not the real social problem in America[2] and if, therefore, those classes should not be studied. One reason that the rich are studied less than the poor is that it is much harder to approach the rich. Difficult and bold as it may be for a middle-class person to knock on slum doors, it is a still greater challenge to get inside a luxury

2. Daniel Bell, in *The Cultural Contradictions of Capitalism*, argues that greed is now the overarching American value.

condominium or a country estate. Imagine how a black teenager from an inner city ghetto would be received if he went from door to door in a white, middle-class suburb, trying to find a family to study.

If you do nevertheless interview a poor person, it may be fair but it is also probably naive to hope that your study might somehow contribute to alleviating the poverty. In the hundred or so years since social scientists began to do "field work" among the American poor,[3] we have had countless studies but few solutions. Knowledge is only the beginning of a solution, and it is therefore inexcusable to interview a poor person as if you were there to help or as if he were part of a social problem. In interviewing anyone, rich or poor, *you* are asking for help, asking to learn and profit from the other person's experience.

Be on guard also against the reverse snobbery, according to which middle-class people are not supposed to be as interesting or colorful as poor people. Even if you think the idea is correct, it is too likely to blind you to the complex and interesting in anyone's life. And you are more likely to be dealing with fresh material if you interview middle-class people, who have been less subjected than the poor to field work by social scientists. Above all, give some peace to dormitory maids, who are possibly the most studied occupational group in America. Get out of the dorm; go off campus and possibly right back to your home town. If you are middle class, you will nevertheless learn about much of interest in the lives of people like you. All that is required is the imagination to look for it.

3. Margaret Mead, in *Blackberry Winter*, reports that her mother researched Italian immigrants in 1902 (p. 35), and earlier instances of such research could probably easily be found.

7

Preparing for the Interview

Though you may be successful in scheduling the interview you want, nothing guarantees that it will be a good one. Like books and movies, interviews should be honest, accurate, and searching, but often are not. Too often, the interviewee is not challenged or not allowed to speak freely because the interviewer does not know enough about the topic to ask intelligent questions or to recognize significant answers. Hence the importance of background research, the next best thing to a time machine, through which you learn about the period or subject in question from sources other than the interviewee.

Background research also enhances your efficiency. Having a limited amount of time with the interviewee, you do not want to spend it learning information that you can acquire elsewhere, before the interview. If you interview an ex-soldier about a battle in which he fought, you do not want to spend the time merely getting an account of what happened. Military histories, newspaper accounts, even movies, will offer versions of what happened. You should be familiar with these versions, and some of your questions should be aimed at finding out if the veteran is in agreement with them. If not, *why* not? If he agrees with the popular versions, then you should aim not only at learning about his particular experiences but also at trying to establish the reasons and emotions that caused his actions. Doing background research makes you well enough informed to get at the interesting, inward stuff of history.

Thorough background research makes it possible to recognize bad answers, dishonesty, or instances of poor memory. Once, when I was interviewing a well-known writer, then in his seventies, about his relationship with another famous person, the writer said he had "never" disagreed with the other person and had "always respected him greatly." If I had done no background research, that would have been the end of that line of questioning. But I had found an article he had written forty years earlier severely attacking the other person. "Did I write that? I'm sorry I did," he responded when I reminded him of the article. As he thought about it, however, he began to remember and defend his reasons for writing the article, recalling disagreements and feelings of hostility and jealousy he had long since forgotten or repressed. The information was very useful, but I would not have gotten it had I not been able to jar his memory with background information.

By putting ourselves in the interviewee's place, we can understand other reasons why background research will make an interview more searching and accurate. All of us are more likely to work hard at accuracy and honesty if the person we are speaking to seems well informed on the issue at hand. This rule applies not only to outright lies but to the petty exaggerations and distortions we might otherwise use to convince ourselves and others that we are better than we are. Then, too, remembering requires effort, sometimes painful effort, which we would be reluctant to make if the person asking us to do so seemed to have gone to little trouble. Conversely, we *are* likely to make an effort when the person interviewing us has clearly already worked hard.

You probably already know the fundamentals of background research, especially if you have done a history paper based on written sources. The library is the place to begin. Get everything you possibly can from printed sources—books, periodicals, government documents, microfilmed newspapers, and so on. If you intend to interview an inventor for a course in the history of technology, learn everything possible about his invention—how it works, the prior technological achievements on which it depends, its social contribution, and the people and machines it displaced. If it is possible to find a written account of the actual invention, read it. If you will be interviewing a writer, read the writer's books. Then read what the critics have said about the books and what the writer has said about the critics. And learn not only about particular inventions and books but also about the broader issues in the field, so that your questions and interpretations can have the broadest possible meaning.

As a general rule, the more famous the interviewee the more that will be in print about him, and the more library research you can do. But don't neglect other possibilities. One interview, for instance, may serve as background research for another. If you are writing about an entertainer who was blacklisted in the fifties for expressing leftist political ideas, it might be useful to interview not only the entertainer but also friends or enemies from that time. Obviously, you have to limit this process somewhere, or else you will be interviewing people who knew people forever. But interviewing someone who knew the entertainer at the time in question could give you a useful outside view, which of course would be just as subjective in its way as the entertainer's own account.

In regard to background research on local celebrities—mayors, judges, educators, clergy, and business and professional people—there will also probably be much printed material, but you may not find it in a college library. You will probably have to visit local libraries, newspaper offices, churches, museums, courthouses, city halls, historical societies, and schools. The places to look for information will be determined by the nature of the person's career. A local politician will probably have been the subject of newspaper stories at election times. From the newspaper, also, you could find out what offices he held and the margin of victory or defeat in local elections. If the politician was a city councilman or mayor, you should look through the minutes of the council meetings if they are available at city hall. Try to get a sense of which issues were particularly sensitive and divisive. Where did the interviewee stand on them, and why?

For ordinary people who are not local celebrities, it is a little more difficult but almost always possible to do background research in written sources. Did the person get married thirty years ago? If you know the date, see if the wedding was covered by the local paper. The account will probably tell at least what the groom did for a living and where the couple planned to live. Be sensitive to the nuances in such documents. Was it a large or small wedding? Did the bride wear a gown or a dress? If the person went to high school, see if there is a yearbook available from that time, perhaps in the school library. What does it say about him? Was he active in extracurricular affairs? If there is a picture of him in the yearbook, does he seem as well dressed as the others? Whatever the factual answers to such questions of nuance, they raise other questions that you may want to address in your interview. Was he as rich or poor, as successful or unpopular, as the documents indicate? And how do those facts affect his perceptions and memories? But this sort of intensive background research on an ordinary citizen can easily become an unjustified invasion of privacy, and if it is to be done very intensively, it definitely requires the interviewee's permission.

It is important, however, to emphasize that such research about ordinary people is possible, because one justification usually cited for resistance to studying the history of the poor and minority groups is that the bottom ranks of society supposedly do not leave useful records. That oral history techniques help make this a fallacious doctrine can be seen by looking at George McMillan's book on James Earl Ray, the convicted assassin of Martin Luther King. Although Ray lived not only at the bottom of society but virtually outside it, McMillan has written a detailed biography based largely on interviews with Ray's relatives, acquaintances, and fellow inmates. But McMillan's research was justified only because the cowardly and treacherous murder of King made Ray something different from an "ordinary" private citizen.

If you intend to use the cultural approach suggested in chapter 4, background research will be useful in establishing the cultural milieu, even if you learn nothing specific about the person you wish to interview. The family, we have said, is a child's first source of culture. But the family probably invented little or none of the culture, obtaining it rather from ancestors and the broader social group. You can acquire knowledge about that generally shared culture from all sorts of sources, including novels, magazines, newspapers, and movies from the interviewee's time and locale. Librarians, clergy, and teachers who have lived in the community for a time are often knowledgeable about such sources, and you may be surprised how much written information is available. The best starting place of all may be a local history society, if there is one. And documents that are not specifically related to your project may still be useful sources of ideas worth exploring in the interview. If you are interested in any medium-sized midwestern town in the 1920s and 1930s, you will find much possibly useful information in the books by Robert and Helen Lynd, *Middletown* (1929) and *Middletown in Transition* (1937), which are based on extensive field work and interviews in Muncie, Indiana. But the ideas you acquire from such sources should remain tentative, and their relevance to your topic should be explored, not assumed, in the interview. For the purposes of oral history, background research in cultural sources will have little point if no effort is made to establish its specific relevance to the interviewee's experience.

This need to place cultural sources in some sort of context, especially the context of social and life history, can be seen in the exciting but finally unsatisfying work of historian Michael Lesy. His *Wisconsin Death Trip*, based mainly on photographs and newspaper clippings from the turn of the century, is an innovative attempt to use qualitative sources to uncover the psychological experiences of ordinary people in a period of economic depression. The result is a gruesome depiction of rural life, replete with insanity, barn burnings, suicides, and murders, and photographs of sad, bored, hating, or terrified faces. Lesy has been criticized on statistical grounds, on the question of whether his relatively small sample of materials accurately represents rural life. But there is no doubt that it represents some of the life experience of some people. The real problem is that, despite the rich images in the photographs and the lurid newspaper clippings, our knowledge remains thin. Not only do we not know in a statistical sense how representative these documents are, we also do not know how well they represent the individuals in them. Nor do the documents establish any useful social context, because they do not shed light on one another: there is no relationship between the documents except for their similar appearance and their common source—one county in Wisconsin.

Admittedly, it is difficult to establish a context on the basis of such anonymous documents reaching back more than eighty years, but in a subsequent book about a more recent time, Lesy has missed an opportunity to use oral history to solve the problem. *Real Life: Louisville in the Twenties* creates a picture of lower-class urban life as dark as that of rural life in the earlier book and this time on the basis not only of photographs and newspaper clippings but also of oral history transcripts. But Lesy did not collect the oral histories himself; he simply dropped them into his book with the photographs and clippings, and the result is that, again, no contextual relationship is established among the documents, and our knowledge remains thin. If Lesy had conducted the oral history interviews himself, with the intention of learning what people who lived through the 1920s in Louisville could make of his photographs and clippings, his book would have had a great deal more coherence. As they stand, both Lesy's books are in a sense all background research, their historical significance undiscernible.

In order to be well prepared for the interview, then, it is

necessary not only to do background research but also to think about how it may relate to the interviewee's experience. Many of the questions you ask should be based on your background research, and you can think about these questions before the interview. Doing so will prevent some, though probably not all, of the why-didn't-I-ask sort of regret that often follows an interview.

You can also think in advance about the order in which you would like to ask your questions. Even though it is a rare interview that develops precisely as the interviewer expects, prior thought about the relationship of your questions to one another will help you guide the interview in the direction you want it to go without seeming to exercise too much control. One obvious and good criterion for ordering questions is the logical relationship among them. This technique may increase spontaneity by making it possible for one question to lead naturally to the next. But another important consideration in ordering questions is the change in the interviewee's attitude between the beginning and the end of the interview, when he will usually be most relaxed and trusting. Therefore, even at the expense of logical order, you should probably plan on saving difficult questions on controversial or personally sensitive material for late in the interview. Clearly, it is in your interest to preserve rapport and spontaneity as long as possible, because, without it, you will get information less thick, less descriptive and detailed. This practice is also in the interviewee's interest, because he will probably best be able to deal with difficult questions if confidence and rapport have already been established by earlier, easier questions. Interviews will seldom end in anger if the interviewer mixes forthrightness with courtesy and respect for the other person's feelings.

There is so much to think about during an interview that, rather than relying on memory, it is useful to prepare a written interview guide containing notes on possible questions in the order in which you would like to ask them. But it is usually a mistake to write out questions in full on the interview guide. Reading a prepared question aloud will make you sound more like a robot than a person and will reduce the spontaneity necessary for a good interview. Instead, jot down a few key words that will serve as a reminder and help you to form the question during the interview. Thus, Amy might wish to ask Senator Shannon about Mayor Daley's personal and political relationship with Adlai Stevenson in the early 1950s. In her guide she should write down something like:

> Mayor's relationship with Stevenson?
> political?
> personal?

Some oral historians recommend, and I have found it a useful practice, making one such note at the top of each page of a stenographer's pad, leaving the rest of the page blank for note taking during the interview. This procedure automatically organizes your notes beneath topic headings. But leave blank pages between questions for notes on unexpected topics, as no open-ended interview will ever precisely follow a prepared guide.

You can also prepare by watching other interviewers at work. Television offers numerous interviews every day, and viewing them with a critical eye is a good way to improve your own technique. But do not model your methods after those of the many television interviewers who are ill prepared, who ask poor questions, or who seem more interested in how they come across on the screen than in what the interviewee has to say. Watch and try to learn from those who are first-rate. Mike Wallace is an excellent interviewer whose questions are always to the point, though as an investigative reporter he tends to treat the interviewee as an adversary. David Frost, always well prepared and desperately curious about the interviewee, probably offers a better example of the sort of intense but cooperative questioning that works best in oral history. When he bought the coveted right to interview Richard Nixon on television in 1977, there were irate protests from American journalists who thought that Frost's background of interviewing entertainers made him ill qualified for a political subject. But his interviewing skills were certainly superior to those of most of his detractors, and in that technical sense the Nixon interviews could not have been much better done. Barbara Walters, who was once a terrible interviewer, has become a fairly competent one. She does not interrupt as often as she once did, and she tends less than formerly to think that she can anticipate the interviewee's answer and supply it in her question. Her progress is proof that interviewing is a learnable skill.

Gathering your equipment together and, if you will be taping, checking to see that the recorder is working well are important aspects of preparation. It should be unnecessary to say that it is poor practice for the interviewer to expect the interviewee to supply paper and pencil for note taking, yet it has happened more than once. Carrying pencils, note pads, recorder, batteries, release forms, and so on in a briefcase or satchel, rather than arriving with your hands full, will help relax everyone, including probably you, most of all.

There are some general guidelines that may help you decide whether you need a tape recorder. You should almost certainly record the interview if you take a preservationist view of your role. That is, if you are collecting the interview for deposit in an oral history collection or for publication, you will want every word to be accurate. Some print journalists are skeptical of the use of the tape recorder in oral history, but they do not understand the need to preserve documents with as much accuracy and integrity as possible. On the other hand, if you, like a newspaper reporter, are conducting the interview for your own writing and expect no further use to be made of the material, a recorder may interfere with spontaneity and be counterproductive. Social scientists who have interviewed without sound recorders have confirmed the accuracy of their notes by having the interviewee check them.[1] Note taking seems especially likely to be accurate enough if the information you hope to obtain is of a hard, factual kind (in the external sense discussed in chapter 1). Yet if you are taking a cultural approach, where detail and thickness are essential, a recorder may be a useful aid to your memory, even if you expect no further use to be made of the interview after you have written your paper. And listening to the tape is the best way to improve your interviewing skill.

If you decide to tape-record the interview, there are some important features to look for in a recorder to make the interview go more smoothly. Cassette recorders are now widely used for interviewing because of their light weight and ease of operation. But if you already own or can obtain a reel-to-reel machine, it will probably produce a better recording. Portable recorders operate on varied power sources: disposable batteries are expensive and do not last long in recorders, and wall current may force you to crawl under a table or

1. See, for instance, Melville Dalton, *Men Who Manage*, p. 277.

behind a sofa in search of an outlet. Plan on using a rechargeable battery, but take along some extra batteries and an extension cord just in case. A recorder with a battery meter will let you check on current flow without playing back some of the tape and interrupting the interview. A remote microphone, rather than one built into the body of the machine, enables you to keep the recorder itself close to you for easy operation. Sound fidelity is enhanced by a "condenser" microphone and flywheel drive rather than belt drive. A "counter" lets you know how much tape is left so that you will know when to turn or change the cassette, though an end alarm serves about the same purpose.

You will need strong, durable tape, because you will probably subject it to much start-stop action while writing your paper. A long-playing cassette will have thin, easily torn tape, so it is best to buy cassettes with no more than a sixty-minute capacity—thirty minutes on a side.

If you are not familiar with the recorder, practice operating it. Learn to load the reel or cassette and to start the machine easily and quickly. Setting up the recorder should not distract the interviewee or subtract from the allotted time. You will also want to be able to be aware of how much tape is left, so that, rather than interrupting, you can change or flip it during a natural break. Practice doing it quickly a few times.

Meanwhile, a few days in advance of the interview, it is a good idea to call the interviewee and remind him of the appointment. I know from hard experience that one can travel far for an interview only to arrive at an empty house or office. This is at least as likely to happen with prominent and busy persons as with ordinary citizens. The interviewee may also be concerned about your faithfulness and will probably be grateful for a reassuring call or letter. Do not count, either, on his remembering the reasons for an appointment made weeks or months earlier. Be prepared to explain your purpose to him in the same general terms you used in your initial letter or contact.

Finally, spend a few minutes examining your own preconceptions, especially those about the interviewee. Most likely, he or she will be old, so try to exorcise any feelings of condescension you have toward the elderly. The myth propagated in our youth-conscious culture of intellectual impairment and bad memory in the aged is only a myth, perhaps entirely false and certainly greatly exaggerated. Psychological tests have shown that the elderly, despite their frequent feelings and complaints to the contrary, often have good memories. It is no more possible to generalize about the intellectual capacities of the aged than to do so about those of any other group. The minds of some may weaken quickly and greatly, but for others it is possible, psychologists say, for growth to continue till very old age. But another cliché about the aged—that they are cautious—is generally accurate and may help explain why they perform far more poorly than the young in situations where there is risk of loss or embarrassment.[2] It is up to you to minimize that risk and help the interviewee perform well by treating him respectfully. By doing so you not only will be acting decently but also will be greatly improving your chances of getting a successful interview.

2. K. W. Schaie, "Translations in Gerontology—From Lab to Life," p. 804.

8
Conducting the Interview

According to communications experts, interviewing is a "transactional," or two-way, process. While Senator Shannon is giving information to Amy, she is also giving information to him. Not only the questions she asks but also her sex, race, age, looks, dress, accent, manners, and numerous other variables help him form an impression of her. And his perception of her will partly, perhaps greatly, determine what he says to her. In short, the experts have discovered what we all know from our personal experience—that what people say depends at least to some extent on whom they are talking to.

The subjectivity of the interviewing situation, which depends not only on your interpretation of the interviewee but also on his or her perception of you, does not necessarily make it an unreliable source of information. But its subjectivity does require that you be sensitive to how you as an interviewer affect the information you get. As in any other field of study, you must interpret the information according to the context in which it is obtained, and in interviewing you are part of the context.

A good example of the way in which the mere presence of an interviewer, no matter how neutral his approach, can bias the interviewee's words is provided by Richard Sennett and Jonathan Cobb in their book *The Hidden Injuries of Class*. But their example also shows that if the interviewer is sensitive and alert to the problem, it need not prevent him from getting reliable information. And in this case, where Sennett and Cobb had higher status than the interviewee, the bias actually helped prove their thesis that a class society is psychologically as well as economically unjust. Reporting on an interview with a group of white working-class women on the subject of racial prejudice, Sennett and Cobb present a four-page transcript of an argument between the clearly bigoted "Dolly" and the seemingly liberal "Myra" and then interpret the argument in this way:

> In this conversation, a hidden, silent authority—the interviewer—had a kind of magnetic pull on Myra: it was at the interviewer that she often looked while she was ostensibly speaking to Dolly, seeking approval for her enlightened views. One of the other women later observed that they had never known Myra to talk this way privately. The change was not so much in her beliefs, Kathy said, as in the manner in which she spoke, the eagerness with which she forced Dolly to announce herself as a bigot. The other women felt betrayed by Myra, seeing her as "putting something on" in an effort to differentiate herself from the rest.
>
> In fastening onto the interviewer's presence, in performing for the outsider to show that she too was educated and "enlightened," Myra had brought to this discussion the weight of a whole lifetime of experience that made her feel obliged to prove she was "worth something" to those "above" her.[1]

In addition to being sensitive about how your presence might be biasing the interviewee's words, you can also to a

1. Richard Sennett and Jonathan Cobb, *The Hidden Injuries of Class*, p. 145.

degree deal with the "transactional" problem by controlling the impression you make on the interviewee. But don't put on an act. Aside from its dishonesty, an act will usually be perceived as such and will, at best, provoke an inhibiting self-consciousness in the interviewee. At worst, it will provoke an act as false as your own. The first rule in interviewing is the same as in life: be yourself. But you should recognize also that you have many ways of being yourself. You behave one way with your parents, another way with friends of your own age, and still another with small children. Each type of behavior is a response to a different social situation. Similarly, in interviewing there are many different possible situations, each of which might require a different type of behavior.

Generally, you should dress and behave in a way that will make the interviewee comfortable. If Amy will be interviewing Senator Shannon in his office, business clothes will probably be best. Such clothes will obviously be wrong for you, however, if you will be interviewing a poor person in his home. Casual dress would probably be best in the latter case, though it should be *your* casual dress rather than an attempt to imitate the clothes of the people in the neighborhood. False appearances are usually recognized and scorned.

The same rules apply to language. Speak the best English you can muster to a well-educated person, while a more casual diction might be better for another interviewee. But in either case speak naturally. If you have been unfortunate enough to acquire any academic jargon, leave it on campus. Plain English will accomplish most of your off-campus purposes. Any attempt to dress up language will seem as false as clothes that are not natural for you. The same thing is true of slang expressions you would not normally use. When William Whyte was doing the field research for *Street Corner*

Society, he found that the street boys resented his efforts to imitate their creative profanity and preferred that he speak in his own natural way. Yet it was true also that the language natural to him in "Cornertown" was different from the language he used at Harvard. He was not acting in either case but simply responding naturally to different situations.

Upon arriving for the interview, be ready to explain your purpose yet again in a friendly, relaxed way that will put the interviewee at ease. Pay attention also to the immediate environment and do what you can to make it conducive to free discussion. Assuming that you are at the interviewee's home, a den or other closed room is best if available. Try to discourage the presence of children and spouse. But no matter what handicaps exist in the situation, deal with them calmly and accept them politely if necessary. Getting flustered will possibly embarrass the interviewee and may be more destructive than the handicaps themselves.

Setting up the recorder efficiently will help give you an appearance of competence and, if you do it unobtrusively, will help relax the interviewee. Keep your attention on him and talk casually while getting ready to record. Putting the machine out of his sight, perhaps under a table or footstool with only the microphone visible on top is a good way to minimize its presence and perhaps also the interviewee's self-consciousness at being recorded. Overheating may result, though, if a bottom-ventilated machine is placed on a carpet. Be sure that *you* can see the recorder and easily check its operation. If the microphone is to rest on a table top or other hard surface, placing it on a folded cloth such as a scarf, or even a magazine or book, will reduce background noise.

Some people will be curious about how they sound on tape, and the quickest way to help them stop thinking about the recorder may be to let them hear themselves. A few may view the recorder as evidence that they are talking to posterity and focus their attention on how they want to appear to future generations rather than on remembering accurately. Informality on your part may help discourage this "You Were There" tendency. But sometimes direct, firm, polite challenges to accuracy are the only way to break down such attitudes. Occasionally it may be necessary to acknowledge defeat and look for another interviewee. Of course you don't admit your defeat to the interviewee: you thank him and depart looking as cheerful as you can.

Taking notes from the very beginning of the interview, even if you are also recording, provides a useful nonverbal way of communicating with the interviewee. Rapid note taking lets him know that you find his words interesting and significant. Your notes also give you something to do and look at during pauses that might otherwise be awkward or make you self-conscious. Note taking helps you to concentrate, to listen, and to remember. Concentrated attention and the pleasure of teaching are the interviewee's principal reward for his effort. Nothing will destroy rapport more quickly than for you to show that you have forgotten or not listened to what he has said.

If you are recording, you may not need to take extensive notes on the conversation, though it is good to remember that your notes will be much more accessible than the recording when you are writing your paper. At least summarize the interviewee's answers and remember also that the recorder will not capture bodily gestures, mannerisms, and facial expressions that help communicate meaning. If any of these seem relevant, be sure to note them. If it is possible to look discreetly at the recorder's counter, you can note the point on the tape where the answer to each question begins—a tactic that may save some labor in writing your paper. If the interviewee uses words or, most likely, proper names you do not know how to spell, circle them in your notes and ask for the correct spellings at the end of the interview.

If you are not recording the interview, notes are doubly important. Write down as much as possible of what the interviewee says. But do not focus so intently on note taking that you cease to be an active listener and questioner. Unless you are an expert stenographer, do not try to write down everything. Bias, your bias, is likely to be introduced into your notes when you write faster than you can actively, critically listen. Try to stay aware of the interviewee as a person, not just a voice, and keep in touch with your own feelings and ideas, distinguishing them from his. Forget about articles (*a, an, the*), conjunctions (*and, or, but*), and other short words except in the rare instances where they are essential. Focus on key words and phrases that carry meaning. You will have to summarize many answers, but even then write down exact words and phrases that strike you as important. Don't forget quotation marks; when writing your paper you will want to know which words are yours and which the interviewee's.

Taking notes also gives you the opportunity to record your own thoughts during the interview. When you want more information on a particular point or if you think of an important question, there is no need to interrupt or risk forgetting. Make a note of the question and ask it at the appropriate moment. Be sure to note also your like, dislike, credulity, or disbelief of the interviewee and his ideas. In addition to making you an active and therefore better listener, writing down your feelings will help you later in thinking objectively about the quality of your relationship with the interviewee. Thinking critically about that relationship is not only essential for an intelligent use of the interview data, it is a good opportunity to learn about yourself.

Good questioning requires good listening. With practice you will develop the mental dexterity needed to consider the significance of a previous answer or to think about what to ask in the next question while at the same time keeping most of your attention on the interviewee. Meanwhile, it is best to err on the side of attentiveness. Careful listening tells the interviewee that you are interested and enables you to probe at the right moment. Be patient even though you will hear much you already know if you have done a good job of background research. If the interviewee seems to be rambling, allow for the possibility that he is getting to the point in his own way. When he does get there, try to understand why he made the transition as he did and what that suggests about his thinking on the question at hand. Be alert for the unexpected detail—you may be at the edge of an important area of information unknown to you. If it sounds possibly interesting and significant, do some exploring. You can always return to your interview guide, so remember that it is a guide, not a straightjacket.

Yet it is up to you to remain in control of the direction that the interview takes. Decide whether or not departure from the direction you expected is justified by asking yourself if you are spending your time well by getting potentially useful information. If not or if you need to stay focused on a special topic, then you should try gently but firmly to get the interviewee back on the subject. Oral history does not mean talking about anything and everything that happened in the past. If it did, you could send the tape recorder and stay at home yourself. The justification for your presence is your role as a critical, helpful questioner aiding in recovering the useful past. The ability to take this active role as tactfully and unobtrusively as possible is the essence of the oral historian's skill.

Silence on the interviewee's part is another large challenge to the oral historian's skill. Moments of silence often make the novice interviewer nervous and too eager to ask the next question, just when the interviewee is finally ready to speak. Remembering takes time, so give it generously. Try to distinguish between the pause that naturally ends a complete thought and the pause that marks a mental search for the right word or detail. Do not interrupt the latter sort. Let the interviewee search his mind while you jot down a note or two. Sometimes silence is a signal, conscious or unconscious, that you have touched on an emotional issue. Letting the silence continue for another moment may prompt a burst of feeling and useful information.

Because you have requested the favor of the interview and because you are there to listen and learn, some deference may be necessary in approaching the interviewee. But deference is easily overdone, especially if the interviewee is a person who seems to want or be used to it. Powerful, prominent people, such as corporation presidents, labor leaders, and politicians like Senator Shannon, are asked so often for their opinions that some of them have lost the gift of candor and frankness. Doctors, lawyers, and teachers have professional relationships with other people that may make them feel more important than they are and more accustomed to deference than is good for them. Some older persons will always talk down to younger ones. Other people may become vain and pompous simply because they are being interviewed. All self-important people are especially susceptible to temptations that Daniel Aaron has well described: "what a person was or did or thought thirty years ago is past and dead, even if that person is technically still alive. The living relic is his own ancestor; and feeling a deep familial piety for his defunct historical self, he indulges in ancestor worship, tidies up embarrassing disorders of his dead past, reverently conceals his own skeleton in a hidden closet."[2] Still other people, clergymen and housewives for example, have social roles that may make them try to edify rather than to recall the way it was. Grandiloquence and false pieties should be challenged early in the interview. Thanks to background research, you should be aware of other accounts and prepared to recognize exaggeration and inaccuracy. Let the interviewee know your preparedness by referring to your background research without being antagonistic or puncturing his self-esteem. Though deference is easily overdone, respect for the other person's dignity seldom is.

The ideal but difficult balance to achieve is that between your own dignity and intellectual independence, on the one hand, and the interviewee's on the other. But it is clear that in the interviewing situation, you should not go to the extreme of defending your ideas by trying to educate the interviewee or correcting his opinions. To do so would contradict the premise of the situation—that he is doing the teaching and that you are there to learn. Deplorable as you may find his ideas, trying to correct them will probably prevent a successful interview. And in any case, unexpected contradictions and lectures rarely convert people; anger is a more likely result. Let your didactic impulses be satisfied with having given the interviewee cause to state his ideas and perhaps to

2. Daniel Aaron, "The Treachery of Recollection," p. 10.

think them through again. By teaching you, he may teach himself. Studs Terkel says that one of the most exciting things that can happen in an interview is to hear the interviewee say, "I never knew I felt that way."[3]

Despite Terkel's weaknesses as a historian, there is no doubt that he is a talented interviewer whose balance between respect for the individuality of the interviewee and understanding of the simultaneous need to reveal his own common humanity might well be emulated by us all. Perhaps he put it as well as possible when he was interviewed on the subject of interviewing:

> One of his [R. D. Laing's] points is that the psychiatrist has to be the fellow-traveler with the patient: that is, he must reveal his own being to the person. That opens up the person, and, in a sense, your own vulnerability. I'm vulnerable, you see. I'm pretty terrible with a portable tape-recorder. [Chuckles.] And sometimes the person, particularly if it's a noncelebrated person—an old lady in a public housing project—will see my tape-recorder isn't working. She'll say: "Hey, it's not working!" And I say: 'No, I goofed." Well, you see, my own vulnerability makes her feel more kinship.
>
> There's a detachment, at the same time, attachment. It's both. You know what they say of Stendhal: He was objective and subjective at the same time; he was outside and inside, both. In a sense, if one could be that—I don't know that I am—but that is the [chuckles] desideratum, whatever. That would be it, that's devoutly to be wished.[4]

So being neutral does not mean that you should be cold or abrupt. Let the interviewee know that you are a human being like him, vulnerable but curious enough to take the risk of trying to understand why you and he have lived as you have.

3. Quoted in Ronald J. Grele, ed., *Envelopes of Sound*, p. 40.

4. Quoted in Denis Brian, *Murderers and Other Friendly People*, p. 291.

Give the interview the semblance of a dialogue, rather than an interrogation, by giving your questions flesh; fill them out with details from what the interviewee has already told you or what you know from background research. If you are enjoying the interview, do not be afraid to communicate your enjoyment and interest when asking questions. Again, interviewing is a two-way process, and the interviewee will warm to his task the more you warm to yours.

9

Asking Questions

Although I have stressed the virtue of courtesy in interviewing, empathy is just as important. You can be completely courteous yet completely miss the interviewee's meaning. Empathy requires the desire and ability to take the interviewee's point of view, and that requires the ability to be objective about yourself. People who cannot face their own weaknesses can seldom tolerate weakness in others. But the good interviewer is not judgmental, at least not during the interview. Feelings of disapproval on your part will often be visible and inhibit the flow of information. An understanding, sympathetic approach, on the other hand, will help establish an encouraging rapport with the interviewee. Rapport, however, can also be overemphasized and produce bias, especially with interviewees who are not naturally critical or introspective.

Experts therefore advise the interviewer to try to develop some emotional rapport but to maintain a neutral stance toward the interviewee's ideas. The best way to accomplish neutrality is through skillfully worded questions that keep the focus on the interviewee's thoughts and feelings, rather than yours, and thus help reduce the complex subjectivity resulting from the interview's two-way, or "transactional," nature.

Because most interviewees will appreciate a prompt, purposeful beginning, it is good to announce that the interview is starting by explicitly identifying the opening question. You can also establish your purposefulness by making the opening question about something the interviewee, in particular, is likely to know. And try to ask the question in a way that will require a detailed answer of some length. Sometimes it is a good idea to begin by getting some background or biographical information about the interviewee, but the opening question should state the main purpose of the interview and require more than a short answer. So you might reassure your home-town social worker that you will come to the point after necessary preliminaries:

> Before we get into social work during the depression, will you tell me a little about your early life and, in particular, what brought you to this town?

Amy, who probably knows much about the senator, might start more directly:

> Now that we can begin, will you tell me about your first meeting with Mayor Daley and the impression he made on you then?

She has made it clear that the interview has started, and by asking in her opening question about *his* meeting with the mayor she has confirmed for Senator Shannon that it is his particular knowledge and expertise that she desires. Better still, she has asked *how* he met the mayor and *what* he thought at the time. If he genuinely intends to cooperate, he will have to answer at length. If Amy had merely asked, "*When* did you first meet the Mayor?" the question, aside from its abruptness and coldness as an opening, would have had the defect of possibly provoking a short answer, such as "1942." Obviously, the interview would have been off to a bad start. Because detail, or thickness, is the special virtue of oral history, the interviewer should ask questions that will produce it.

Another advantage of provoking a detailed answer at the outset is that the interviewee's own words can then be used to form succeeding questions that are not "leading." Though leading questions may not introduce as much bias as is commonly thought,[1] they should usually be avoided early in the interview. For instance, Senator Shannon may answer Amy's opening question by saying that his first impression of Richard Daley was of a warm, friendly young man, not at all as "ruthless and cold blooded" as he had heard from "others." Amy's background research may cause her to think that the "others" were a particular group in the local Democratic party. But putting the question that way might predetermine an answer according to political categories. If political questions were not involved in the dislike to which the senator has referred, leading his thoughts in that direction will be a mistake and may prevent Amy from finding out what was really on his mind. So she uses his own words to ask her next question:

Who were the "others," the ones who thought he was "ruthless and cold blooded?"

The extremely leading or "loaded" question is the best and most notorious example of how an unskillful interviewer can

1. Stanley Payne, *The Art of Asking Questions*, p. 179; William W. Cutler III, "Accuracy in Oral Interviewing," p. 4.

prejudice the information he gets, not because he will mislead the interviewee but because he may mislead himself. If Amy admires Mayor Dalcy, she should nevertheless not ask Senator Shannon,

Wasn't the mayor a *wonderful* man?

The question not only is vague but is "loaded" with the view that the mayor was wonderful; it asks the senator not to give his own opinion but merely to confirm hers. No one likes to appear critical or negative, so even if the senator disliked the mayor he may not express his true feelings. The danger is probably especially great in situations where the interviewer has higher status than the interviewee. Presumably, that is not the case with Amy and the senator, but even in Amy's situation the strength of the answer may be mitigated out of courtesy. Worse still, because her question asks for a positive answer, she may mistake a noncommittal response for "yes." The difficulty with loaded questions is not that they produce false answers but that they produce answers difficult for the interviewer to interpret accurately, because his own subjective bias is so heavily involved in the original question.

Occasionally, however, background research will have turned up information different from the interviewee's account, and you may wish to see how he responds to the opposing argument. In these circumstances a *negatively leading* question can be useful, but the challenge should probably not seem to come personally from you. Instead of countering the interviewee's idea with an assertion of your own, put it in the form of a question and report it as the opinion of a third person. To take an extreme example, Amy might ask the senator:

What do you think of Peter Yessne's book, *Quotations from Mayor Daley*, which makes the mayor seem stupid and tyrannical?

The senator's response is likely to be voluble. If he agrees with the book's idea, mention of it will encourage him to express his own negative feelings. If he disagrees, he may be provoked, perhaps angrily, to defend the mayor. Because negatively leading questions usually get the interviewee to talk at length, some oral historians encourage their use.[2] But they have not thought critically enough about the two-way nature of the interview. Several negative questions, even if reported as the opinion of third parties, may cause the senator to view Amy as especially receptive to critical information about the mayor. Once that happens, he may become either defensively sullen or unreliably opinionated, depending on his own prior attitude. So negative questions should not be used simply because they are provocative. Be alert and self-disciplined enough to reserve them for situations where they serve an intellectual purpose, such as finding out how the interviewee will deal with opposition.

You should of course honestly tell your own opinion to the interviewee if he insists on knowing it. But he may not insist, because as David Riesman once pointed out, being interviewed has become a widespread social rite in America.[3] The interviewee will probably understand and enjoy having the entire conversation focused on his ideas. And he is still more likely to stay focused on his ideas without asking for yours if you communicate empathy through a nod of the head, an affirmative mumble, or a noncommittal statement, such as, "I see what you mean."

2. Willa K. Baum, *Oral History for the Local Historical Society*, p. 20.
3. David Riesman, *Abundance for What?* p. 539.

Sometimes a defensive interviewee will ask a rhetorical question, aimed not at finding out what you think but at putting you in your place. You can often answer such a question with another question, showing that you do know your place as learner, not teacher, in the interview situation. The following exchange might take place between Amy and the senator about the ethics of the Democratic political machine in Chicago:

Senator: The political machine didn't take advantage of minorities and immigrants. Don't you think the foreign-born should be helped in a new country?

Amy: So that was the machine's main function? Helping minorities and immigrants?

By asking another question that shows she is willing to be taught, she may make him comfortable enough to launch him on the topic of what he sees as the machine's justifying social role.

Still, the interviewee may justifiably demand to know the opinions of the person to whom he is giving so generously of his own ideas. Although telling him your opinion violates the experts' injunction to be neutral, it may possibly be more harmful to refuse. Such a request may amount to a plea that you join in a search for the meaning of the experience under discussion, and a refusal may seem like an expression of disinterest in the interviewee's life. But if your opinion differs from the interviewee's, try to prevent the disagreement from becoming personal. Let him know that you respect his opinion: "If I were in your position, I might have felt the same way." This kind of statement may also serve the useful purpose of returning the focus as quickly as possible to the interviewee's thoughts and ideas.

Follow-up, or "probing," questions that ask for elaboration or explanation of a previous response are crucial to getting detailed information. Their importance is proven by their absence and the consequent weakness in television interviews, where questioners often feel pressed for time and skip from one topic to the next without follow-up questions. The result is a failure to challenge interviewees at crucial points. "What *is* the national interest,"' one sometimes longs to hear a politician asked.[4] But in an oral history interview based on mutual cooperation in exploring the past, follow-up questions must be skillfully asked in order to avoid giving the interview a "third degree" quality. Avoid questions like "Will you define that word?" or "Can you be more specific?" Get the answers indirectly, without challenging the other person. If Senator Shannon says "most people" were glad to see the mayor win an election, Amy should not ask, "Then why was it so close?" Instead, she should try to learn the meaning of "most people" with a question like "So he had strong support that year?" In cases where the interviewee's ego might be threatened, a preliminary assurance that you will not react critically may be useful even though somewhat leading. Amy might encourage the senator to describe honestly his feelings while campaigning in a dangerous neighborhood by saying:

I would have been frightened in such a situation. Was fear a problem?

As the interview progresses and rapport is established, shorter follow-up questions or merely encouragement may provoke elaboration. When the information is good and you want more, be generous with expressions of interest and grati-

4. Studs Terkel colorfully expounds this point in Ronald J. Grele, ed., *Envelopes of Sound*, p. 19.

tude—"Just what I need to know," "That's interesting," and so on.

Leading questions are likely to be less harmful near the end of the interview than at the beginning, and they may even be necessary if the interviewee has been uncooperative or simply unable to remember. Once you have made an effort to get unbiased information and to form an opinion of the interviewee's reliability, leading questions may help elicit information in greater depth and detail. Amy, knowing from background research that Mayor Daley made an important decision on 9, 10, or 11 January, has tried to learn which by asking the nonleading question "Do you remember the date?" and has received the unsatisfactory answer "No." Therefore, she now resorts to a leading question, but one that states all possibilities:

Could it have been January 9th, 10th, or 11th?

Asking if it was the ninth and leaving out the possibility that it was the tenth or eleventh could produce bias. The senator, finding the ninth reasonable enough, might confirm the date rather than reveal his inability to remember. You the interviewer, once having decided to lead, should do so as neutrally as possible by stating alternatives in your questions. Revealing your own lack of certainty is the best way to help the interviewee deal honestly with his.

Sometimes background research can be used to help the interviewee's memory. Rather than asking if it was 9, 10, or 11 January, Amy might ask if the decision was made before or after an important city council meeting, which the newspaper says occurred on the afternoon of the tenth. Referring to concrete details and events will often help the interviewee be more specific about abstractions like dates. After Amy has ascertained the senator's ideas, and only then, she might ask him to pass judgment on her interpretation:

> Do you think that the council meeting might have influenced his decision?

And later, when Amy interprets and weighs the significance of the answer to such a question, it is crucial for her to remember that the senator has only passed judgment on her idea rather than stating his own. A terse "Maybe" is as good as a denial. But if he has excitedly said, "Oh yes, I remember now . . ." and begun a long answer, it may be full of important information.

Even when the focus of the interview is on subjective feeling and attitudes rather than objective fact, background research can still be very useful. Asking for the source of a feeling or attitude is usually unsuccessful, because most people do not think along such lines. But by reading a newspaper quotation to the interviewee or showing him a photograph or other material document, the interviewer can help him relive an experience and remember what he felt during it. Such questions are most successful when they call specifically for introspection and when they are couched in the past tense, which explicitly asks the interviewee to ignore later ideas and rationalizations in favor of what *he* felt *then*:

> Looking at the photograph of these people and thinking back, how did *you* feel while standing in the relief lines?

The above dos and don'ts of asking questions are not meant to be hard and fast rules but guidelines to be adapted to the situation you find. All the above suggestions are based on the assumption that you have never before met the interviewee and that no relationship has been established at the beginning. But if you are interviewing a friend or relative whom you have known for years (and who knows you and your ideas well), it would be silly and affected to be neutral: better then to engage in a frank, probing exchange of ideas of the sort you might normally have with a friend or relative, as opposed to an "interviewee."

Sometimes, too, a warm relationship will develop during an interview or, most likely, a series of interviews, and it might be foolish as well as unworthy not to acknowledge that relationship in the way you ask your questions. Martin Duberman, while researching his book about Black Mountain College, interviewed a couple who had been students there in the 1930s. During the interview, which lasted for two days, Duberman's attitude shifted from dislike to warm respect and trust. Here is an excerpt from the transcript, a discussion of an incident in which two male and two female students violated an unwritten rule against "mixed "overnight trips together:

DUBERMAN: So then what do you do with the right of dissent, such as these four students exercised—going against the "sense of the community"?

MORT STEINAU: It boiled down to, "How much are you as an individual contributing to the community? How much is your disturbance of the community a negative thing?"

DUBERMAN: Rather than a positive act of conscience?

MORT: That's right. . . . It was the cumulative effect of attitude probably as much as anything else. It wasn't so much what you did but how you did it. . . . Certainly, there were boys and girls taking walks in the woods. What transpired no one ever knew except those two. If they were in general good members of the community no questions were raised. . . .

DUBERMAN: Don't you think . . . that concern over "public reaction" was used by some members of the faculty as a pretext to cover their own puritanism?

MORT: I would say that there is much in this. . . . But this was a family. And what one's brothers and sisters and uncles and aunts were doing was on everybody's mind . . . in this community, the college rules extended throughout the vacation.

DUBERMAN: We're on . . . central stuff . . . I mean, the whole tension between how you could simultaneously be an individual, which was the whole point in many ways of Black Mountain, and yet be a responsible member of the community.

BARBARA STEINAU: . . . If you're a member of a group that's already dissenters, can you really dissent and can you really revolt? . . . they dignified the whole thing by not even having a vote, so that it's worse if you go against it than if it was a vote.

DUBERMAN: Well, I would think that would encourage maturity, because you would then have to say to yourself, "Look, they've allowed me some leeway as an individual to go against majority opinion. And so I'll have to be that much more sure in my own mind that I really want to do this, that it's important to me as an individual to go against the majority. . . .

BARBARA: . . . I have the feeling that it was a community for mature people . . . those who were not sufficiently mature needed some rules, even some rules to break.

DUBERMAN: But if there are no actual rules, but merely a "sense of the community," it's a little bit harder to be a rebel.

MORT: Some people are licked by this lack of definition. . . .[5]

Duberman is violating several of the guidelines suggested in this chapter by ceasing to be neutral, by leading the interviewees, and by asking for their ideas *now* as well as their feelings *then*. Yet far from being a bad interview it is obviously an exciting intellectual experience. He has formed such a high regard for the Steinaus' reliability and thoughtfulness that rather than viewing them merely as sources he sees them as historians themselves and is asking for their interpretation of Black Mountain College as a community, the central theme

5. Duberman, *Black Mountain*, pp. 94–95.

of his book. Obviously too, they understand the challenge and are equal partners in the investigation. When they disagree with him they are able to resist his leading questions because they understand that his questions are only his contribution to a joint effort.

But not all interviews can be conducted so happily, and to prove the point it is only necessary to look at another excerpt from Duberman's book. Trying to get information about the poet and teacher Charles Olson, Duberman interviewed Michael Rumaker, another former Black Mountain student. This time Duberman might have done better by following some of the guidelines in this chapter. Here is part of the interview:

MICHAEL RUMAKER: . . . He [Olson] loved to talk . . . everybody loved to sit at his table because he would just hold everybody rapt . . . and he was always available. One of our first misunderstandings occurred when one night—Charles had a large appetite and loved to eat and so forth, and this was the last table that hadn't been cleared yet, and I was washing the dishes and I wanted to finish off the dishes so I could get back to my study and do some work. And I sent my helper into the dining room to get Olson's dishes from his table, and I heard Olson yell out, "I'm more important than any fucking dishwasher!" Which was true I suppose. I was very hung up on—very meticulous about—doing my job right, because I was afraid they were going to send me back to the farm. But what I should have done was said, "The hell with it," and just close down the kitchen and go and let the dirty dishes sit there. But I had to finish my job, you know. And it hurt me then, but I think about it now and I think it's funny. He's right.

DUBERMAN: I don't think he's right.

RUMAKER: What he had to say was more important than getting those damn dishes done.

DUBERMAN: He could have done both—he could have sent the dishes in, and gone on talking.

RUMAKER: That wasn't Charles's way. He was a law unto himself in a sense, and not badly so. He was a man who had his own quirks and his own idiosyncrasies. . . .

He could talk a blue streak; he's a brilliant talker.[6]

Here Duberman is not merely leading but is contradicting the interviewee. It is not clear what he thinks he is accomplishing by so strongly inserting his own views into the discussion, but he clearly is not furthering his aim of learning about Olson. By so harshly judging Olson's action, Duberman misses the point that Rumaker saw some redeeming quality in it, though exactly what we never learn, because Duberman does not ask, as he should have, "Why was Olson right?" Instead, he contradicts Rumaker so flatly as to silence him except for a brief defense of what he has already said. Then Duberman defends his contradiction. It is Rumaker who finally brings the focus back to Olson as teacher and talker, the theme in which Duberman is ostensibly interested.

An admirable desire for honesty and personal engagement of the kind Duberman enjoyed with the Steinaus probably lay behind his actions. But tactics like those he practiced with Rumaker achieve personal involvement and self-exposure for the interviewer at the expense of denying the interviewee the chance to express his thoughts and feelings. Such behavior has been characterized by the sociologist Richard Sennett as typical of novice interviewers who have a laudable desire to treat interviewees as fellow human beings, not just research subjects. Sennett adds, however, that eventually novice interviewers "begin to see that, exposing themselves, they are losing the opportunity to find out about the subject's feelings. This opportunity will arise if the interviewer asks questions,

6. Ibid., pp. 380–81.

or just sits silent, waiting for the other person to go on. After a time, sensitive interviewers begin to be uncomfortable with the idea that to treat someone else as an emotional equal you must have a reciprocal relationship with him. . . . Boundaries around the self are not isolating but can actually encourage communication with others."[7] In short, if Duberman had been more self-restrained and used a more neutral approach of the sort suggested in this chapter, it would have been more productive, not only in obtaining information but in the human relationship between him and Rumaker. Neutrality, properly used, expresses interest, not disinterest, in the interviewee's experiences and ideas.

7. Richard Sennett, *The Fall of Public Man*, p. 10.

10
After the Interview

After an hour or perhaps two of talking and remembering, the interviewee will probably be tired, and you almost certainly will be if you have worked hard at asking good questions, listening well, and taking notes. But there is still much to do.

A person not used to being interviewed may want reassurance that he has done well. Staying for a few minutes and showing a personal interest as well as gratitude for the interview is a good way of reinforcing a vulnerable ego. Use this time to check spellings of which you are not certain and to ask if the interviewee knows of or owns background material such as photographs, scrapbooks, or diaries kept by family members. If so, you might try to borrow them to check against the interview or to prepare for another meeting if there is to be one. Also, if you were dissatisfied with a particular answer, this is a good time to bring up the question one last time. Inhibitions are sometimes loosened once the recorder has been shut off and the interview formally ended.

It is important to "write up," as anthropologists say, your overall ideas and impressions while the interview is still fresh in your mind. If you are more than an hour away from home, try to find an uncrowded restaurant where you can order a cup of coffee or a soft drink and have a table at which to work. Go over your notes, using them to stir your memory and adding details you were too busy to write down at the time. Then begin writing as searchingly and introspectively as if you were making a diary entry. As in taking notes, "writing up" is a chance to focus on your own ideas as well as the interviewee's. But now you should focus on larger questions: How successful was the interview? Was the interviewee apparently cooperative and reliable? Were there trouble points where things might have gone better? Be self-critical. How might you have affected the information you got? Did the interviewee seem consistent or contradictory, and what in particular caused your impressions? If you will interview him again, do you have new ideas for questions, unresolved areas in which you want to probe further? How does the interview seem to relate to your project as a whole? Does it suggest possibilities for further research, either in the field or in the library?

If you did not tape-record the interview, use the time just afterward to expand your notes. It is sometimes asserted that the interviewer's memory is too precarious to be trusted without a tape recording[1]—a position obviously inconsistent with the heavy reliance placed on the interviewee's memory. Some oral historians are among these skeptics, perhaps because the remembrances of the interviewer are so dissimilar to traditional archival materials. The transcript of a tape recording, on the other hand, has one strong resemblance to letters, diaries, and other traditional manuscript sources—it

1. John A. Neuenschwander, *Oral History as a Teaching Approach*, pp. 22–23.

contains the interviewee's own words. But a written summary by an interviewer is also a document, and though presenting more difficult problems in interpretation for later scholars, it may well be useful archival material. An unrecorded interview is certainly preferable to no interview at all. But if you did not use a recorder, you should immediately after the interview produce a whole new set of expanded notes. Begin again on clean paper but with your old notes close at hand, using them to stimulate your memory, to preserve the topical order of the interview, and as a source of quotations. The goal is to write down everything you can remember that the interviewee said and thus come as close as possible to what the transcript of a sound recording might look like. In many instances this will still involve summarization of answers. But in other cases you may be able to remember exact words or to fill in gaps between quotations in your old notes. Do not hesitate to do so if the memory is strong and clear; many of the quotations you read in history texts resided only in someone's mind for hours or days before they were set down on paper. Summarize or quote your questions and synchronize them with the interviewee's answers. Leave room in the expanded notes for later additions. Memory sometimes improves in the short run, and you possibly will be able to expand the notes still further in a few days. Neat, short paragraphs will make the notes easier to read later, and if you plan to send the notes to the interviewee for verification, you should type them.

If you recorded the interview, listen to the entire tape within a few days of the interview and decide whether or not to transcribe it. Oral historians recommend doing so because a transcript is more accessible to future scholars. Although listening to a tape will require at least as long as the original interview, a transcript may be scanned in a fraction of the time. But transcription requires from six to fifteen hours for each hour of tape and may therefore be too laborious and wasteful if you expect to be the only person using the tape. Referring directly to the sound recording while writing may be more efficient, though it will probably require some tedious start-stop action to find the segments you want. Of course, there are possible compromises between the extremes of a complete transcript or no transcript at all. You might transcribe only the parts of the tape that sound as though they may be useful sources for your written paper. Or you might outline the tape, indexing it according to the recorder's counter in order easily to find the segments you need while writing:

Tape 1, side 1
0–40 first meeting with mayor
41– "others" hostile to mayor
64– mayor's personality discussed
91– recalls mayor's reminiscences of childhood

Outlining or indexing will probably be best for students who plan to make no further use of the tape after writing the research paper.

But one of the potential rewards of oral history research is that after your paper is written there may quite possibly be some further use to be made of the interview. A librarian or archivist in a college, university, or local historical society may be happy to add the transcript of your interview to its collection. If so, then you will have the satisfaction not only of having engaged in genuinely original research but of knowing that your efforts have saved something for historical knowledge that might otherwise have been lost. Furthermore, the sheer human interest of many oral history documents often makes them publishable. Depending on the nature of the material, a local newspaper, scholarly journal, or university or company magazine may be interested in publishing your interview. Again, you will have escaped the sense of futile exercise that accompanies too much student research. But before attempting to arrange for publication or deposit in an oral history collection, read Chapter Twelve, "Matters Legal and Ethical." And you will need to make a transcript.[2]

Writing down or typing what you hear on a tape recording may at first seem like a mindless activity, but in fact it is a critical exercise. To transcribe is to translate language from one medium to another, from speech to writing, while attempting to preserve as much of the original meaning as possible. The difficulty is that much of what gives speech its meaning cannot be duplicated on paper—inflection, stress, pace, volume, accent, and the sound of words themselves. Just as the letters of the alphabet, differently combined, are a symbolic device for representing individual sounds and words, it is necessary to find ways to represent other aspects of speech.

Punctuation is one such device, but its use in transcription does not always follow the rules of grammar, where, for instance, a period is supposed to mark the end of a complete sentence. Though people may write complete sentences, they do not always speak them. In talking, people leap from one topic to another, leave one sentence uncompleted, and push another on till the end seems unrelated to the beginning.

2. For many of the thoughts on transcription in this chapter, I am indebted to the excellent brochure by Mary Jo Deering and Barbara Pomeroy, *Transcribing without Tears*.

Because respect for the integrity of the oral history document usually forbids "correcting" it, your guideline for inserting periods will have to be not the rules of grammar but rather accuracy and fidelity to the interviewee's intentions. Where does he seem to complete one thought and begin another? In other words, you will have to make an interpretive judgment based mostly on the sound and content of the interviewee's words. Though the resulting sentences might sometimes horrify a grammar teacher, their meaning will nevertheless usually be clear. Your use of commas, colons, dashes and other punctuation marks should be governed by the same general rule of respect for accuracy of meaning rather than grammar.

Some sophisticated attempts have been made to develop a system of written signs that would represent the sounds of speech with much greater precision than is accomplished by merely adding punctuation marks.[3] But these systems are laborious for both the transcriber and the inexperienced reader, and it seems very unlikely that the required investment of energy is repaid in historical dividends. Any user interested in verbal behavior should listen to the recording rather than read the transcript. If you think that your recording may be of verbal interest, try to deposit it in an oral history collection that saves recordings as well as transcripts.

Many characteristics of speech are easier to describe than to symbolize. Brackets ([]) separating your words from the interviewee's are a convenient way to insert description into the text. If it seems important that the interviewee speaks laughingly, emphatically, angrily, quickly, softly, or tearfully,

3. See, for instance, Dennis Tedlock, "Learning to Listen: Oral History as Poetry," in Ronald J. Grele, ed., *Envelopes of Sound*, pp. 106–25.

provide such adverbs in brackets just before the speech they describe. Brackets can also be used for description of non-verbal behavior, such as gestures, though you will have to recover these from your notes rather than the recording. In general, the inclusion of such description in brackets can easily be overdone and should be reserved for instances where it has a significant effect on meaning. Variations in accent or dialect due to class, region, or ethnic background may be interesting, principally for biographical reasons, but they are probably best described in a prefatory note to the transcript. Changes in spelling to symbolize a slow dra-a-wl or a nasal twang-g-g quickly become tiresome to readers.

You can also make the transcript more readable by breaking it into short paragraphs, by completing confused or dangling sentences in brackets, and by using footnotes to make factual corrections. Intelligent paragraphing requires listening ahead for several minutes at a time to find natural breaks:

AS HEARD

Well to make a long story
short Martha liked that house in
town and so we bought it we
were eager to move in right
away for all sorts of reasons
the rainy season was coming
soon and the roads would be
muddy I wanted to sell the livestock while prices were up and
Martha was pregnant so I told
Jones who was selling us
the house I told him I would
give an extra fifty dollars to be
out by the end of the month but
he . . .

AS TRANSCRIBED

Well to make a long story
short, Martha liked that
house in town, and so we
bought it.

We were eager to move in
right away for all sorts of
reasons. The rainy season would
be coming soon, and
the roads would be muddy. I
I wanted to sell the livestock
while prices were up.
And Martha was pregnant.

So I told Jones, who was
selling us the house, I told him
I would give an extra fifty dollars
[to him] to be out by the end of
the month. But he . . .

Dangling or confused sentences can be made readable by adding your own words in brackets, as in the example above and also in the following case:

AS HEARD	AS TRANSCRIBED
We weren't being vengeful we simply thought that in the interest of justice retribution and really we were very lenient	We weren't being vengeful. We simply thought that, in the interest of justice, retribution [was necessary]. And, really, we were very lenient.

If you are too unsure of the interviewee's intended meaning to complete his sentence for him, use a dotted ellipsis:

We simply thought that in the interest of justice, retribution . . . And, really, we were very lenient.

Finally, when the interviewee is not sure of his facts or else your background research shows that he has made a mistake, perhaps because of loss of memory, provide additional information or correction in a footnote rather than changing the text:

I went to my first radical meeting in Berkeley in the summer after my freshman year. I think it may have been an early SDS meeting.* Anyway, it turned out to be . . .

———

*The summer after her freshman year would have been 1959—before Students for a Democratic Society was founded.

Whether to change or delete any of the interviewee's words is the most difficult issue in transcribing. Some oral historians are opposed to any changes other than punctuation and paragraphing. A few critics, apparently more interested in verbal behavior than history, are opposed to transcription itself! Both are minority positions and likely to remain so. A good oral history interview is conducted for an intelligent purpose that may include preservation. If so, the interviewer and transcriber, doing their utmost to preserve the interview's integrity, are also obligated to help make it accessible to future users. Therefore, though it would be wrong to correct and thus misrepresent the speaking style of a consistently ungrammatical interviewee, you might for the sake of readability correct a rare slip in a generally grammatical account, especially if the interviewee has corrected it himself on tape:

AS HEARD	AS TRANSCRIBED
He gives gave I mean a lot of money to charity	He gave a lot of money to charity.

Nothing significant is lost by the correction, and the transcript is easier to read because of it. But sometimes a self-correction is made for a reason other than grammar and, because it adds to meaning, should be allowed to stand. For example, the ironic intention in the following sentence should not be lost:

That year I earned my living by substitute teaching, baby-sitting I mean, in the local high school.

Some deletions are easy to decide upon. "Uh" is probably the most commonly spoken monosyllable, often used unconsciously by even the most fluent speakers while mentally reaching for the right word. Except in the rare instances where "uh" adds something to meaning (perhaps by suggesting nervous hesitation), there is no point in reproducing it in the transcript. The same is true of false starts where the interviewee might begin, "He . . . ," then reject the construction in mind, and start again: "You see, there was a great deal of pressure on him from the South Side. . . . " If the interviewee leans often on crutch phrases, such as "you know" and "you see," there is little point in including them all, though some should be retained in order to represent his speaking style. Including many crutch phrases, false starts, "uhs," coughs, sneezes, and so on in the transcript will only give it the appearance of gibberish and make reading it difficult, exasperating work.

Because transcription is essentially an editing process, the authenticity of the transcript can only be assured by returning it to the interviewee for final checking. If the interviewee wants to make changes he certainly has the right to do so, and you should welcome changes as long as they increase accuracy and clarity. It is also acceptable for the interviewee to save himself embarrassment by striking out profanity or substituting "yes" for the "yeah" to which many people resort in speaking. But spontaneity of language is one of the means through which an interview achieves its meaning. So try to discourage much cleaning up of diction, grammar, and syntax, which if carried too far will make the transcript seem stilted and unnatural. Explaining that the transcript *should* look rough and spontaneous, compared to a finished piece of writing, may provide enough reassurance to keep the interviewee from overediting.

Include your questions in the transcript. Future readers sensitive to the two-way nature of interviewing will want to know not only what the interviewee said but also what he was asked. Therefore, the transcript should have a question-and-answer format:

Q: Did the mayor ever talk about his parents?
A: Yes, he seemed to have an especially fond memory of his mother. He told me once that she . . .

Including questions in the transcript also focuses your attention on your performance as interviewer. Listening critically to that performance may often be painful, but it is an important step toward improvement and self-knowledge. Listen carefully to your questions and try to understand why some work better than others. If the interviewee becomes tense or uncooperative, could you have helped provoke his behavior? Are you courteous, and do you sound like an enjoyable person with whom to talk? The tape recorder has partly satisfied the wish of the poet:

O wad some Pow'r the giftie gie us
To see oursels as others see us!

PART FOUR

11
Writing the Paper

The process of writing history involves interpreting documents. Before and during the writing you have to decide what your research has taught you. Therefore you have to think critically about the evidence you have collected. If you have already written a traditional term paper, you will find that the critical questions about oral documents resemble those about written. The principal difference is that, in the case of the oral document, the critical questions are often more personal and subjective because of your involvement in creating the document. The consequent difficulty in interpreting the oral document can be both frustrating and excellent training. The problem is that, though an interview may contain lies, it is unlikely to contain *the* truth. The best that you can hope for is that the interviewee has told *a* truth, the truth as it looks to him. Your crucial critical question, therefore, is not "How do I know that the interviewee has told the truth?" Rather, you should ask,

> What do I know from the interviewee's words about his actual experience and about his perception of that experience?[1]

1. For this and several other ideas in this chapter I am indebted to

In answering these questions there are several different kinds of evidence to consider.

External evidence, that is, background information collected from some source other than the interviewee, is the best check on the overall reliability of the oral document. In researching my biography of Van Wyck Brooks, American literary critic (1886–1963), I interviewed several people whose letters to Brooks of forty, fifty, or even sixty years earlier I had already read. When their recollections squared with events and emotions expressed in their earlier letters, I tended to give credence also to parts of the interview where there was no external corroboration. If their recollections were not consistent with the earlier letters, I usually accepted the testimony of the written documents and discounted the interviewee's general reliability. But it is easy to imagine a case where an earlier written document would not be as reliable as the oral history interview. Senator Shannon could have written a letter for ulterior political purposes, but, years later, he might feel free to disavow it in order to speak his mind honestly. In weighing a spoken document against a written document, much attention must be given to the situation in which each was created.

Internal evidence refers to the logic and consistency of a document, considered alone. Consistency is an especially useful test of factual accuracy. Consider, for instance, the case of a survivor from a town struck by tornadoes on two successive days. If he has told you that he left town after the first tornado and has then described the second, his inconsistency has given you a reason to distrust his accuracy that background

---

J. P. Dean and W. F. Whyte, "How Do You Know If the Informant is Telling the Truth?" in Lewis A. Dexter, *Elite and Specialized Interviewing*.

research will be unlikely to overturn.

But in dealing with subjective feelings and motives, as opposed to external facts, consistency should not be too strictly demanded. Mixed or even opposing feelings are common. A man may one moment be bitter as he recalls having had to work his way through school and the next moment say that the experience was good for him. Both statements may be equally honest and accurate expressions, not only of his feelings during the interview but also of what he felt then.

Logic is sometimes the best internal test of feelings and motives. If the survivor of the tornadoes has said that he left town immediately after the first tornado in order to avoid the second, you have logical grounds to suspect his accuracy; one tornado is not automatically followed by another. Such an explanation may be a later, unconscious rationalization of a more shameful motive, such as panic. On the other hand, if you were alert enough during the interview to ask him why he expected the second tornado, he may have told you that there was a radio warning. But if he did not mention a warning and you have found no indication of it in your research, the internal evidence would suggest that you should distrust his recollection of motives.

Implausibility is a possible test of any document, oral or written. Some actions or events are so rare or unlikely to happen that disbelief is a natural response to accounts of them—miracles, for one example, and flying saucers, for another. Sometimes events plausible in themselves may be rendered implausible by the circumstances in which they are supposed to have occurred. The report of a rape during a college class provokes skeptical questions: what were the professor and other students doing—conducting class as usual?[2] But the charge of implausibility is neither a logical nor an empirical test. It is simply a statement that such things do not happen in the world you know. Because no one knows the world perfectly, the implausible may be possible and true. Keep an open mind, check background research, and be prepared to discover gaps in your own knowledge. If in the end you reject an account as implausible, recognize that the rejection is a statement not merely about the account but about your own knowledge and understanding of the way things are.

The *Personal Quality* of the document's creator, the interviewee, is also a valid question. Does he strike you as trustworthy? Do his spoken attitudes square with other observations you can make about him? If he claims not to be interested in material things, for instance, does the kind of house he lives in seem to support or contradict him? What about his general attitudes? Would they tend to discredit something he has said? An obvious bigot might be a reliable source for many kinds of information but probably not on matters involving people of a different race or religion.

The best interviewee will often show some healthy skepticism about his memory but will at the same time have a sense of history, an understanding of the importance of the past to the present. Comparing the words of Blackie Gold, a car dealer, to those of Cesar Chavez, the farm labor organizer, would suggest that the latter is likely to be a better source for oral history:

GOLD: "I've never brought up the Depression to my children. . . . Why should I? . . . there's no reason for it. They don't have to

2. Dexter, *Elite and Specialized Interviewing*, p. 126.

know from bad times. All they know is the life they've had and the future that they're gonna have.

CHAVEZ: Some people put this out of their minds and forget it. I don't. . . . I don't want it to take the best of me, but I want it to be there because this is what happened. This is the truth, you know. History.[3]

Finally, the *Relationship* between you and the interviewee requires attention yet one more time. Are you likely to meet again socially, with resulting embarrassment for the interviewee if he was utterly candid? Or are you likely to meet someone else who knows him—his employer, perhaps? If so, might he have distrusted or hoped to use you? And don't forget to think once again about the immediate situation of the interview. As far as you can tell, what was the interviewee's idea of you, and how might it have affected what he said? How successful were you in being neutral? Did he learn or already know any opinions or ideas of yours that might have affected his answers? Again, the point is not that his answers might be invalid but rather that interpreting the meaning of his words requires interpretation also of the situation in which he spoke.

Having thought critically about the evidence and arrived at your interpretation, you should devote a fairly large proportion of your total time on the project to writing. You will probably find it helpful if before and during the writing you can discuss your ideas with your instructor and perhaps even submit to him a preliminary report on your research. Some of your best ideas will emerge *while* you write. If you have already written a term paper, you know that it is hard work

3. Studs Terkel, *Hard Times*, pp. 184–90.

and that you will probably have to go through at least two drafts before you can begin to express your ideas clearly. Remember that the best-written, most interesting history re-creates the past, not documents. Your paper should be the result of your research, not just a description of it. *Use* documents to support *your* ideas. Stay focused on your argument and on presenting as clear, convincing, and lively an account as possible.

Structuring the paper so as to reveal some of the possible connections described in Part Two among life history, culture, and society could be an effective way of enhancing its interest. If you are writing about the experiences of a member of your family during the depression, your research has probably led you from the particular to the general, from, say, your uncle's experience to the broad social forces and events that affected his life. Reversing that direction in your paper by moving from the general to the particular is a good strategy for gaining the attention of a reader who does not know your uncle. For the reader does know about the depression and knows that it has had at least some influence on the direction of his own life. By moving from the forces that produced falling crop prices to the foreclosure of your uncle's farm, you show the effect of national history upon an individual person, a human being like the reader. Most of the paper may be focused on your uncle's experience of unemployment in the city, but by quickly sketching in the broad forces that produced this situation you can set it in historical context and heighten its significance for readers.

The format of your paper need vary little from that of previous papers you have written, especially if you are using oral history in the way suggested earlier—as one source among others in a more or less traditional term paper. One change you will need to make is the easy one of finding a footnote form for interviews consistent with that for written sources:

Thomas J. Shannon, interview with author, 21 December 1979, Chicago.

In other respects, however, the format may be the same as in any other paper, with you presenting your ideas in the text and giving quotations, from either the interview or other documents, to support your points.

When referring to the interviewee in the text, it is usually best to call him by his name (or pseudonym if you are protecting his identity). "Interviewee" is stiff, academic jargon and is used justifiably only in situations, as in this book, where the "interviewee" is an abstraction. There are other words that could be used in place of "interviewee," but they are even less satisfactory. "Narrator" is a good word but does not capture the give and take of the interview situation. "Source" is too impersonal. So is "subject," which might also be confused with the topic of your paper. "Informant" is too close to the pejorative "informer." And "witness," which has a nice religious ring in one context, may sound legalistic in another. Luther Evans, former Librarian of Congress, proposed "oral author," but this term, like "narrator," fails to suggest that an interviewer has also actively helped to create the document.

You may have to make some changes in your writing style, changes caused principally by your personal involvement with the oral document. Though you have probably been urged to use "I" as little as possible in essays and term papers, the first person may be useful in quoting an interviewee whose words are best understood as a response to your specific question. "I asked" is certainly preferable to "the interviewer asked" or some other impersonal phrase. Of course, you can sometimes avoid the first person by quoting in a question-and-answer format. But it may still be necessary to analyze or relate some aspect of your personal involvement in the interview, and it will sound more natural in the first person. But the fundamental principle remains true that unnecessary involvement of yourself in the account will seem egotistical and intrusive.

Another difference between a paper based on oral history and a traditional term paper results from the relative inaccessibility of the oral document to your reader. When you cite a written document, especially a book or periodical, your reader can look it up and soon know as much about it as you know. Therefore, you owe it to your reader to describe your research in some detail, either in the text of the paper or in an appendix stating:

1. How you found the interviewee and who he is
2. How you interpret the impact of his general attitudes or frame of mind on his response to your particular questions
3. Your assessment of your relationship with the interviewee and its effect on what he said
4. Your background research and any other checks you made on the accuracy of the oral document

Your description of your research should probably be written in the first person, and it may be nearly as important and interesting as the rest of the paper. Because you cannot tell everything, keep it reasonably short. Focus on the critical questions that have been most challenging and difficult for you while working with the documents. If the interview transcript is to be given to a library or oral history collection, include the description of your research as an appendix to the transcript, because it may be useful to future historians in interpreting the document.

12
Matters Legal and Ethical

A person's unpublished words are his legal property and should not be used without his consent, or his executor's consent if he is dead. In order to save future researchers the difficult, often impossible, task of finding the heirs of an interviewee and getting permission to publish, oral historians usually ask interviewees to sign a release, deeding or giving ownership of the interview to the oral history center, subject to whatever restrictions the interviewee may impose. Usually, after a stipulated date, the center in turn will be free to open the material to historians who want to quote for publication.

Oral historians are considerably more cautious than journalists, the most prolific interviewers, who routinely identify themselves and then assume that consent to publish is implied by the very act of speaking to a member of the press. Oral history often generates more sensitive personal information—what newspeople would call privileged, or off the record—which is one reason why oral historians make no such assumptions about publication.

Using oral history in a term paper, however, may not require a formal release. If you make it clear from the beginning that an instructor will be reading parts of the interview, you have fulfilled your obligations to the interviewee. Still, it is a good idea to save copies of your correspondence, and if you are tape-recording, to get the interviewee's assent on tape.

If you have hopes of publishing your paper or the interview itself or of contributing it to an oral history collection, a written release will be necessary. Your editor or the director of the oral history center will not only require one but may provide a standard form. If not, type your own form, keeping it short and simple, as in the following example:

Release Form

The sound recording and transcript of my interview with ______ on the date of ______ may be used by him for such purposes as he sees fit, including publication or deposit in an oral history collection for public inspection.

______

______

(signature)
(date)

Some interviewers recommend that the interviewee be asked to sign the release *before* the interview. The potential advantage for the interviewer in such a procedure is clear. Time should not be wasted by a capricious person who later decides he did not want to be interviewed. But the advantage may be offset by the potential disadvantage that the release may inhibit responses. As usual in oral history, there is no rule that applies to all cases, but, more often than not, the release is signed at the end of the session.

When you ask the interviewee to sign a release, keep the process simple and informal. Don't be legalistic about it. Above all, do not let it make you an adversary. If it is honest to do so, present the release as a formality that you and the interviewee, as sensible people with more important things to think about, should settle quickly. Offering to protect identities by changing names will sometimes persuade a reluctant interviewee to consent to publication. But it ought to be clear that he has every right to prevent publication if he has not signed a release.

Even if the interviewee has signed a release, publication without his knowledge raises some difficult questions. After all, people not used to being interviewed may be drawn into greater frankness than they had thought possible. Among scholars I have heard disturbing stories about publication, sometimes recounted as if they were triumphs, centered on circumventing the wishes of interviewees. If you think your interview contains important material but cannot persuade the interviewee to permit publication, there is always the possibility of depositing it in a library under "seal," in the hope that a future heir or executor will be more cooperative. (This means a large research library, since smaller ones are not usually able to accept restricted material.)

A release does not absolve you of all legal responsibilities, especially for publishing libel. If someone is unjustifiably hurt by publication of the interview, you may be as accountable as the interviewee. *The American Heritage Dictionary* defines libel as a "written, printed, or pictorial statement that damages a person by defaming his character or exposing him to ridicule." Legal definitions of libel vary from state to state, but you do not need a precise legal definition if you follow the usually sensible rule of not publishing anything that might damage a living person's reputation. The only possible exception would be if the information were relevant to the public good. For instance, the acceptance of a bribe by a public official would merit public discussion. But before publishing such information, consult an attorney. Furthermore, the acceptance of a bribe will probably not be proven by a single oral history interview, so unless corroborated by other sources, such a story is best suppressed. This does not mean that you should erase the tape or scissor the transcript. You could deposit the tape and transcript in an oral history collection, "sealing" them for a stipulated number of years until all principal parties are likely to be deceased. The accusation may be a lie, but even lies are useful to historians, if only for what they say about the liar.

For students, subtle ethical questions, rather than the particular legalities of publication, are most likely to prove troublesome, and they can arise at any point in the process of researching and writing. Although Amy will want to be as persuasive as possible in trying to get Senator Shannon to grant her an interview, there are clear ethical bounds to her aggressiveness. He owes her the courtesy of an answer to her request, and she would be justified in writing several letters, telephoning, or going to his office without an appointment if that is what is required to get an answer. And because he is a public figure, she may be justified in not accepting "no" as an answer the first time around. But she would surely not be justified in trying to get him to give in by making a nuisance of herself in his office or badgering his secretary. All these cautions are doubly true in the case of a private citizen, who should have to say "no" only once.

Keeping promises is an obviously ethical practice but not always an easy one to maintain, especially if you are too generous with promises at the outset. If you are not sure that you will transcribe, do not promise the interviewee a transcript. Once you have promised, transcribe even if it later seems unnecessarily tedious. Luring someone eager for attention into granting an interview by raising expectations of publication when you are not sure it will be possible is an obviously bad practice.

Intensive background research, especially on private citizens, raises ethical problems already briefly discussed in Chapter Seven. But the point bears repeating that such research should not be conducted without the permission of those involved. And even with general permission to do background research, you should have specific, written permission before looking at bank, medical, and school records, which are sometimes surprisingly accessible even though they are supposed to be private. Specific permission should also be obtained before conducting interviews with friends and acquaintances of an ordinary private citizen with the intention of learning about that individual. In any case, it is unlikely both that the person in question would agree and that the intellectual return would justify the time and energy invested.

Furthermore, doing background research for a project not related to any particular person may still turn up possibly destructive information. One student studying the social role of her home-town high school telephoned a now prominent "graduate" of the school to ask for an interview. During the conversation he became nervous and wary. It was soon obvious both that he had not finished high school and that he did not want anyone in the community reminded of that fact. The student wisely kept the information out of the paper and did not even reveal the man's name in seeking advice about the matter.

A more subtle invasion of privacy can occur if the interviewer does not have a serious purpose but is simply using the interview as an excuse to meet someone, famous or otherwise, in whom he is interested. Friendships *can* arise from the interviewing situation; I first met a good friend through an interview. But it is *unlikely* that a friendship will be struck up in a one- or two-hour meeting. Resentment at being unnecessarily disturbed is a more likely response than friendship if it becomes evident that the interviewer is unprepared and uninterested in the ostensible subject.

Neither should the interviewer aspire to the rôle of psychological therapist in the course of one or two meetings, even though the need for meaning and catharsis may make the interviewee willing to explore bad memories. Bad memories should be explored if they are relevant, but whether the interviewee is helped or harmed by the interview may be hard to determine and is mostly his affair. Until he indicates differently, the interviewer is obligated to maintain the strictly historical purpose that was his original justification for intruding in another person's life.

If you feel bad or guilty about asking for sensitive information, it may be best for both ethical and practical reasons not to ask for it. It is usually pointless and possibly destructive to ask a question in a tone that conveys apologetic feelings. Yet in attempting to resolve your feelings, you should not forget your obligation to your own integrity as a historian. Interviewees often recognize the need for that integrity and receive hard questions more calmly than you might expect. As with much else about interviewing, decisions have to be made on the spot, as you acquire an understanding of the situation in which you are working.

Some students may be disturbed by the idea of maintaining a neutral stance while asking the interviewee to be self-revelatory. And careful, tactical planning for the interview may seem manipulative and dehumanizing. These are difficult questions for many researchers, and there are no easy answers. But you should certainly not let any of the guidelines suggested in this book cause you to behave unethically or antisocially. Interviewing is inevitably a two-way social process, and the idea of neutrality is not to abolish but only to reduce the interview's complex subjectivity, in order to increase communication and understanding by making interpretation easier and more accurate. In situations where neutrality seems too cold or inhuman, it may also be counterproductive. You want to get information that is thick and rich in detail as well as accurate, and neutrality should not be carried to the point of inhibiting the interviewee.

Yet the ethical standards you bring to interviewing, though high, should not be unrealistically higher than those guiding other parts of your life. Like most people, you probably find that social standards, mere kindness, or the economics of your personal energy supply require that at times you quietly accept rather than explain a difference with another person, even at the risk of giving him a mistaken impression of your ideas. In the interview situation, your goal of minimizing the influence of your ideas in order to see the other person's as clearly as possible is respectful of his identity and, in that sense, humanistic. And the interviewee, by allowing himself to be interviewed, has tacitly agreed that his experiences and ideas, not yours, are up for discussion. Interviewing in general as a research technique, because it depends on voluntary cooperation, is at least in little danger of violating the interviewee's right to privacy.

Probably the most sensitive issue likely to arise after the interview is confidentiality. If you do not do your own typing, your typist should be a responsible person with no conflict of interest, no grudges against the interviewee. The same goes for your teacher. If he or she is not such a person, write another term paper on a different subject. Perhaps most difficult of all is the frequent, seemingly unimportant temptation to talk with friends and teachers about interesting information. The interviewee deserves better than gossip for his pains, and sensitive information given you for a term paper or other serious purpose should not be the subject of loose talk.

Finally, some commentators have suggested that the mere act of writing about and interpreting the interview—in a term paper, for instance—raises ethical questions. Instead of writing about and analyzing the interview, they say, it is better simply to reprint it, letting the interviewee's words speak for themselves. According to this line of thought, interpretation amounts to the statement that the interviewee's life can only have significance if his words are viewed as representative "of some greater issue of which that person is merely a convenient example." In this way, analysis is supposed to involve the implicitly political statement that the interviewee is not as significant a human being as the interviewer. By simply reprinting rather than analyzing the interview, the political terms of the relationship become more equal—"a contract essentially of friendship, of mutuality, and not merely one of questioning and answering":

> The person's life, or really the tiny fragments he or she gives *me* . . . represent the entirety of the inquiry. . . .
>
> This is why the actual words become so important and why no further objective analysis is left to be undertaken. It is research based on esthetic judgments and human intuition, both fundamental ingredients of the dramatic or dramaturgic. One seeks to know how life is led.[1]

1. Thomas J. Cottle, *Private Lives and Public Accounts*, p. 35. Robert Coles has expressed similar ideas more briefly in his Afterword to Dorothy Gallagher, *Hannah's Daughters*, p. 340.

One does seek to know how life is led, but one knows already that it is not led in a vacuum. It is led in the context of culture and society and history, and if the interviewee's words are not viewed in that context they *do* lose significance, including political significance. They especially lose significance for a third person, the reader, who does not know the interviewee personally and who therefore does not share in the "contract . . . of mutuality" described above. The reader has an infinite number of possible ways of spending his time, many of them potentially more significant than reading the words of a person he does not know. To say this is not to say that the reader is a better human being than the interviewee but only that the reader is a different human being, one among billions. To justify the reader's attention, the interviewee's words must have some special claim. One claim, of course, may be the sheer interest, literary interest perhaps, of the words themselves. But that interest is in no way reduced and much is gained if the words are implicated in history where the reader also lives. Sometimes that analysis is first done by the interviewee himself. What makes *All God's Dangers* such a satisfyingly coherent book, complete in itself, is Nate Shaw's power of historical imagination. He not only tells his story but views it in the context of, and assesses its significance for, "this Southern way of life." Yet even if the interviewee does engage in analysis himself, his account remains a particular historical document, no more unique than any other, to be weighed against others in the reader's imagination if nowhere else. There is always interpretation, and to assert that the interpretation of you the writer is unethical because it *is* interpretation is tantamount to saying that the interview should never have taken place.

13

Oral History Collections and Sources

Even if you decide that your term paper topic does not require that you do an oral history interview, you may still be able to use oral history documents collected by someone else. Directors of oral history centers agree (and complain) that the tens of thousands of interviews in their collections are underused. Many scholarly books are published every year that would have been the richer for research in oral history collections. Sometimes this neglect occurs simply because researchers remain unaware of the existence of collections relating to their topics. If you are undertaking a research project in twentieth-century American history, it is possible, indeed likely, that there is relevant material in an oral history collection somewhere.

To find that material, turn to *Oral History Collections*, by Alan Meckler and Ruth McMullin. This book, which should be but is not always in the reference collections of large libraries, indexes the holdings of many of the more than four hundred oral history collections in existence in the United States as of January 1974. Interviews are indexed by name.

They are also indexed by subject, such as aeronautics, Indians, moving pictures, or New Deal. A second section of the book describes in general the holdings and major research interests of oral history centers, indicating whether or not the center will make its interview transcripts available through interlibrary loan or by microforms.

If a copy of *Oral History Collections* is not immediately available, there are other finding aids. *Oral History in the United States: A Directory*, compiled by Gary Shumway, provides terse descriptions of most of the oral history collections then in existence and carries a useful index. Since 1971 the annual volumes of the *National Union Catalog of Manuscript Collections*, which will be found in any sizable library, have listed major oral history collections and indexed individual memoirists in them. In addition, some oral history projects published detailed catalogs of their collections, which may be available in your library or in a nearby oral history center.

The best news for students about oral history collections is that parts of some of the more significant ones have begun to be microfilmed and may already be available in your library. Hundreds of transcripts from Columbia University's huge collection are now available on microfilm, including interviews of people prominent in art, business, education, international affairs, labor, law, literature, politics, religion, and science. Other microfilmed collections focus on the history of jazz in New Orleans (collected by Tulane University), civil rights (Stanford), American Indians (University of South Dakota), contemporary Jewry (Hebrew University), and pioneers of the movie industry (American Film Institute). A complete listing of oral history on microfilm is available from The New York Times Oral History Program, New York, New York, 10036.

Scarcely a week goes by without publication of a new book of oral history. Some are scholarly in approach but nevertheless popular—for instance, Oscar Lewis's *Four Men*, a richly detailed account of the impact of the Cuban revolution. Others, like *What Really Happened to the Class of '65?* by Michael Medved and David Wallechinsky, are produced for the mass market. But whatever the author's intentions, such books are almost inevitably both useful to the serious student and interesting as human documents. They offer both enjoyment and insight, and, when they are relevant to research interests, you should not hesitate to use them as primary sources.

You can find such sources in about the same way you would any other book. Check with faculty members acquainted with the field. Look in the subject index of the library card catalog and in indexes to periodicals and scholarly journals. The *Newsletter* of the Oral History Association and also its *Oral History Review* are good sources of information on recent books and developments. So is the annual report published by the Columbia University office, where sound-recorded oral history began. It is free for the asking and includes a listing of other useful publications, available individually or in kits.

Still another useful source of oral history is the work of collectors who were active before the invention of the tape recorder. One of the largest and most famous collections of oral history interviews (although they are not called that) is composed simply of written summaries by the interviewers. These are the more than two thousand interviews of ex-slaves conducted by the Federal Writers' Project from 1936 to 1938. All the interviews have been reprinted in a nineteen-volume series entitled *The American Slave*. But the potential usefulness of the collection is weakened by the fact that most of the ex-slaves interviewed in the 1930s were still children when they were liberated in the 1860s and could not give first-hand accounts of what it was like to be an adult slave. Also, the interviewers and their editors were naive and occasionally dishonest. It has been proven that they doctored some transcripts to produce thicker accents than they heard and that they sometimes tried not to give "some damn Yankee, even today, a good excuse to complain of the treatment accorded to Negroes in those days."[1] Most of the interviewers were honest, but they were also mostly white and did not understand that their color often provoked distrust and calculation among the ex-slaves. The following sort of exchange occurs all too frequently in the collection:

> "Well, what about the Yankees? . . . Were you glad that they set you free?"
> "I suppose dem Yankees wuz all right in dere place," she continued, "but dey neber belong in de South. . . . An as for dey a-settin' me free! Miss, us niggers on de Bennett place was free as soon as we wuz bawn. I always been free."

Another interviewer writes: "When asked about slave days, he gets a faraway expression in his eyes; an expression of tranquil joy."[2]

Yet the interviews of ex-slaves are a useful source if subjected to the same critical questions you should ask about interviews you conduct yourself. Background research is possible in the numerous slave narratives printed about the time of the Civil War, such as Frederick Douglass's, though many of these narratives, too, had untrustworthy editors and must be used cautiously. A small but probably more reliable collec-

1. Quoted in Ken Lawrence, "Oral History of Slavery," p. 85.
2. George Rawick, ed., *The American Slave*, pp. 221, 312.

tion of interviews with ex-slaves was gathered by blacks at Fisk University in the late 1920s, and they (also reprinted in *The American Slave*) are useful not only in themselves but as a standard against which to evaluate the Federal Writers' Project interviews. By reading the FWP interviews carefully, you can make some deductions about how much bias was introduced by one interviewer in contrast to another. The fact that the interviewers were mostly *white* women is regrettable, but the result would probably have been worse still if they had been white *men*. There is an ambiguity in many of the accounts that a "transactional" analysis would suggest may actually be a canny subversiveness. One old woman graphically describes how a slave, albeit "de meanest nigger boy I eber seed," was tortured and hanged by a brutal mob of whites and, concluding the story, says to her interviewers, "But all and all, white folks, den was de really happy days for us niggers." And because of the inhibiting circumstances, the few ex-slaves who speak angrily must be given special weight: "When slavery was goin' on it was all right for me 'cause I never had it hard, but it jes' wan't right to treat human bein's dat way. If we hadn't a had to work an' slave for nothin' we might have somepin' to show for what we did do, an' wouldn't have to live from pillar to pos' now."[3]

Interviews of poor whites in the South were also collected by the Federal Writers' Project, and a volume of them, *These Are Our Lives*, was edited by W. T. Couch and published by The University of North Carolina Press. Recently, a new volume of the FWP interviews, *Such As Us*, edited by Tom E. Terrill and Jerrold Hirsh, was published by the same press. This collection is an attempt to present some of the best and

3. Ibid., pp. 324–25, 388.

most representative accounts of both black and white interviewees. It also contains a fine introduction, the most sophisticated attempt yet to place the interviews in the contexts both of the 1930s, when they were collected, and of the southern cultural and social history to which they speak.

The interviews that historians since Herodotus have collected for their own books are still another possible source of oral history. To cite a slightly more recent example, Josiah Royce's *California*, first published in 1886, uses a large number of oral history documents, many of which were collected by another scholar, Hubert Howe Bancroft. Copies of many of the "statements" by early settlers that Royce used are still on file in the Bancroft Library at the University of California at Berkeley. The most interesting interview in the book, however, is the one Royce conducted himself in 1884 with General John C. Frémont. As a young army captain in 1846, Frémont had instigated the Bear Flag Revolt, still too often viewed as a heroic uprising against Mexican oppression. The revolt was in fact both unjustified morally and unnecessary from an imperial point of view, because the Mexican War would have brought California into the American fold anyway.

Frémont's supporters said that Bear Flag was justified because of an imminent Mexican attack, but Royce's background research showed there had been no such danger. In the interview, Frémont did not mention the threat of an attack but offered what seemed a more reasonable explanation—he had been given a secret mission by the U.S. government to seize California. The story of the impending attack had apparently been concocted at the time of the revolt to placate domestic public opinion, which required that America be the injured party rather than the aggressor in California. But Royce did not stop there. He located in State Department archives the secret dispatch that Frémont said authorized the use of force and found that it urged peaceful measures! Frémont had either lied or been mistaken, not only at the time of Bear Flag, but also during the interview thirty-eight years later.

What, then, did Royce learn, if anything, by interviewing Frémont? The answer is precisely that "inner" or cultural meaning of events which, as I earlier suggested, oral history is likely to help reveal. Just as Frémont implied in the interview, the greedy urge to conquer California had been the motivating force, though he had either lied or unconsciously attempted to shift responsibility from himself to the U.S. government. At the time of the revolt, however, Frémont had found it expedient to identify himself more closely with his country and had therefore, according to Royce, persuaded his followers and perhaps himself that an attack by the Mexicans was imminent. The innermost lesson of the episode had to do with the "American character": "The American wants to persuade not only the world, but himself, that he is doing God service in a peaceable spirit, even when he violently takes what he is determined to get."[4]

Because of Royce's thoroughness, his account in *California* of his interview with Frémont would still be a useful document to a historian or student who wished to investigate the question of Bear Flag for himself. Royce, of course, did not have a tape recorder, but he took extensive notes during the interview and later submitted them to Frémont for correction. The resulting account of the interview in his book is as trustworthy, if not as complete, as a transcript of a recorded

4. Josiah Royce, *California from the Conquest in 1846 to the Second Vigilance Committee in San Francisco*, p. 151.

interview submitted to the interviewee for correction. The same is true of the work of many nineteenth-century and earlier historians who used interviews as source materials.

In determining, however, the worth and usefulness of oral history collected by others, there is need for just as much care and thoughtfulness as in using an interview you conducted yourself. And the critical questions are the same. Where and when did the interview take place, and how might those circumstances have affected what was said? Can you determine the nature of the relationship between interviewer and interviewee? Did either of them have an interest to protect? Is the oral account consistent with background research? If not, which source seems strongest, and how do you account for the discrepancy? In one case, a frail memory may have obscured the past, and in another, the passage of time may have allowed an individual to speak more honestly than previously. Or, as in the case of Royce and Frémont, perhaps only more background research will enable you to fathom the significance of an interviewee's statements. The answers are inward and therefore assure the largest possible test of your imagination.

Acknowledgments

This book was written during time made available by the program for Andrew W. Mellon Faculty Fellowships in the Humanities at Harvard University during the 1977–78 academic year. Richard Hunt and Katherine Kozack of the Mellon program at Harvard made the year there pleasant as well as profitable. Daniel Aaron was also a generous host. I am especially indebted to the Harvard undergraduates who patiently used an early draft of this book as a text in a course I taught in the fall of 1977. Without the encouragement of Malcolm Call, Editor-in-Chief of the University of North Carolina Press, I probably would not have revised the manuscript for publication. Louis Starr and Jacquelyn Hall offered many useful suggestions from their perspective as professional oral historians. Jack and Jane Censer suggested several useful sources. George McMillan added the insights and criticisms of a journalist. Paul D. Escott led me to sources on aging and memory. Linda Burcher made suggestions on style and helped prepare the manuscript for publication. The confidence and support of Carol Aberbach Hoopes were essential. Responsibility for errors is mine alone.

Bibliography

There is already a very large body of literature on oral history, as well as an enormous amount of writing on interviewing. Therefore I have restricted the list below to works mentioned in the text or cited in the notes. Students needing to read beyond this list will surely not be numerous, and they will find additional bibliographies in many of the works listed below.

Aaron, Daniel. "The Treachery of Recollection: The Inner and Outer History." In *Essays on History and Literature*, edited by R. H. Bremner, pp. 3–27. Columbus: Ohio State University Press, 1966.

Baum, Willa K. *Oral History for the Local Historical Society*. Stockton: Conference of California Historical Societies, 1969.

Bell, Daniel. *The Cultural Contradictions of Capitalism*. New York: Basic Books, 1976.

Benison, Saul. "Oral History: A Personal View." In *Modern Methods in the History of Medicine*, edited by Edwin Clarke, pp. 286–305. New York: Oxford University Press, 1971.

Blythe, Ronald. *Akenfield: Portrait of an English Village*. London: Penguin, 1969.

Brian, Denis. *Murderers and Other Friendly People: The Public and Private Worlds of Interviewers*. New York: McGraw-Hill, 1971.

Brown, Richard D. *Modernization: The Transformation of American Life, 1600–1865*. New York: Hill and Wang, 1976.

Charlton, Thomas. "Oral History in Graduate Instruction." *Oral History Review*, 1975, pp. 65–66.

Coles, Robert. *Children of Crisis: A Study of Courage and Fear*. Boston: Little, Brown, 1964.

Colman, Gould P. "Oral History—An Appeal for More Systematic Procedures." *American Archivist* 28 (January 1965): 79–83.

Cottle, Thomas J. *Busing*. Boston: Beacon, 1976.

———. *Private Lives and Public Accounts*. Amherst: University of Massachusetts Press, 1977.

Couch, W. T., ed. *These Are Our Lives*. Chapel Hill: University of North Carolina Press, 1939.

Cutler, William W. III. "Accuracy in Oral Interviewing." *Historical Methods Newsletter*, June 1970, pp. 1–7.

Dalton, Melville. *Men Who Manage*. New York: Wiley, 1959.

Davis, Cullom; Back, Kathryn; and MacLean, Kay. *Oral History: From Tape to Type*. Chicago: American Library Association, 1977.

Deering, Mary Jo, and Pomeroy, Barbara. *Transcribing without Tears: A Guide to Transcribing and Editing Oral History Interviews*. Washington, D.C.: George Washington University Library, 1976.

Dexter, Lewis A. *Elite and Specialized Interviewing*. Evanston, Ill.: Northwestern University Press, 1970.

Dollard, John. *Criteria for the Life History: With Analyses of Six Notable Documents*. New Haven: Yale University Press, 1935.

Duberman, Martin. *Black Mountain: An Exploration in Community*. New York: Dutton, 1972.

Gallagher, Dorothy. *Hannah's Daughters: Six Generations of an American Family, 1876–1976*. New York: Thomas Y. Crowell, 1976.

Garner, Van Hastings. *Oral History: A New Experience in Learning*. Dayton, Ohio: Pflaum, 1975.

Geertz, Clifford. *The Interpretation of Cultures: Selected Essays*. New York: Basic Books, 1973.

Gluck, Sherna, ed. *From Parlor to Prison: Five American Suffragists Talk about Their Lives*. New York: Random House, 1976.

Grele, Ronald J., ed. *Envelopes of Sound: Six Practitioners Discuss the Theory, Method and Practice of Oral History and Oral Testimony*. Chicago: Precedent, 1975.

Haley, Alex. "Black History, Oral History and Genealogy." *Oral History Review*, 1973, pp. 1–25.

———. *Roots*. Garden City, N. Y.: Doubleday, 1976.

Hamburger, Robert. *Our Portion of Hell: Fayette County, Tennessee: An Oral History of the Struggle for Civil Rights*. New York: Links, 1973.

Harris, Ramon I.; Cash, Joseph H.; Hoover, Herbert T.; and Ward, Stephen R. *The Practice of Oral History: A Handbook*. Glen Rock, N.J.: Microfilming Corporation of America, 1975.

Hodes, Art, and Hansen, Chadwick, eds. *Selections from the Gutter: Portraits from the Jazz Record*. Berkeley: University of California Press, 1977.

Joseph, Peter. *Good Times: An Oral History of America in the 1960's*. New York: Charterhouse, 1973.

Lawrence, Ken. "Oral History of Slavery." *Southern Exposure* 1, nos. 3 and 4: 84–86.

Lerner, Daniel. "Interviewing Frenchmen." *American Journal of Sociology*, September 1956, pp. 187–94.

Lesy, Michael. *Real Life: Louisville in the Twenties*. New York: Pantheon, 1976.

———. *Wisconsin Death Trip*. New York: Pantheon, 1973.

Lewis, Oscar, et al. *Four Men—Living the Revolution: An Oral History of Contemporary Cuba*. Urbana: University of Illinois Press, 1977.

Lifton, Robert Jay. *Death in Life: Survivors of Hiroshima*. New York: Random House, 1967.

Lynd, Robert, and Lynd, Helen. *Middletown*. New York: Harcourt, Brace, 1929.

———. *Middletown in Transition: A Study in Cultural Conflicts*. New York: Harcourt, Brace, 1937.

Maccoby, Michael. *The Gamesman: The New Corporate Leaders*. New York: Simon and Schuster, 1977.

McCoy, F. N. *Researching and Writing in History*. Berkeley: University of California Press, 1974.

McMillan, George. *The Making of an Assassin: The Life of James Earl Ray*. Boston: Little, Brown, 1976.

Mead, Margaret. *Blackberry Winter: My Earlier Years*. New York: Simon and Schuster, 1972.

Meckler, Alan M., and McMullin, Ruth. *Oral History Collections*. New York: R. R. Bowker, 1975.

Medved, Michael, and Wallechinsky, David. *What Really Happened to the Class of '65*. New York: Random House, 1976.

Mintz, Sidney. Foreword to *Afro-American Anthropology: Contemporary Perspectives*, edited by Norman E. Whitten, Jr., and John F. Szwed. New York: Free Press, 1970.

Montell, William Lynwood. *The Saga of Coe Ridge*. Knoxville: University of Tennessee Press, 1970.

Moss, William W. *Oral History Program Manual*. New York: Praeger, 1974.

Neuenschwander, John A. *Oral History as a Teaching Approach*. Washington, D.C.: National Education Association, 1976.

Payne, Stanley. *The Art of Asking Questions*. Princeton: Princeton University Press, 1951.

Rae, John. "Commentary." *Technology and Culture*, Spring 1963, pp. 173–76.

Raines, Howell. *My Soul Is Rested: Movement Days in the Deep South Remembered*. New York: Putnam, 1977.

Rawick, George, ed. *The American Slave: A Composite Autobiography: Alabama and Indiana Narratives*. Westport, Conn.: Greenwood, 1972.

Riesman, David. *Abundance for What? And Other Essays*. Garden City, N. Y.: Doubleday, 1964.

Roddy, Joseph. "Oral History: Soundings from the Sony Age." *Rockefeller Foundation Illustrated*, May 1977, pp. 2–7.

Rosengarten, Theodore. *All God's Dangers: The Life of Nate Shaw*. New York: Knopf, 1974.

Royce, Josiah. *California from the Conquest in 1846 to the Second Vigilance Committee in San Francisco: A Study of the American Character*. Boston: Houghton Mifflin, 1886.

Schaie, K. W. "Translations in Gerontology—From Lab to Life: Intellectual Functioning." *American Psychologist*, November 1974, pp. 802–7.

Sennett, Richard. *The Fall of Public Man*. New York: Knopf, 1977.

———and Cobb, Jonathan. *The Hidden Injuries of Class*. New York: Knopf, 1972.

Shumway, Gary. *Oral History in the United States: A Directory*. New York: Oral History Association, 1971.

Solzhenitsyn, Alexandr. *The Gulag Archipelago: An Experiment in Literary Investigation*. New York: Harper and Row, 1974–78.

Spradley, James; and McCurty, David. *The Cultural Experience: Ethnography in Complex Society*. Chicago: Science Research Associates, 1972.

Starr, Louis M. *Oral History*. In *Encyclopedia of Library and Information Science*, vol. 20. Reprint. New York: Oral History Publications, Oral History Research Office, Columbia University, 1978.

Stein, Jean. *American Journey: The Times of Robert Kennedy*. Edited by George Plimpton. New York: Harcourt, Brace, Jovanovich, 1970.

Terkel, Studs. *Hard Times: An Oral History of the Great Depression*. New York: Pantheon, 1970.

———. *Working: People Talk About What They Do All Day and How They Feel About What They Do*. New York: Pantheon, 1974.

Terrill, Tom E., and Hirsch, Jerrold, eds. *Such As Us: Southern Voices of the Thirties*. Chapel Hill: University of North Carolina Press, 1978.

Vansina, Jan. *Oral Tradition: A Study in Historical Methodology*. London: Routledge, 1961.

Whyte, William F. *Street Corner Society: The Social Structure of an Italian Slum*. 1947, Reprint. Chicago: University of Chicago Press, 1955.

Wicker, Tom. *A Time to Die*. New York: Quadrangle, 1975.

Wigginton, Eliot, ed. *The Foxfire Book*. Garden City, N. Y.: Doubleday, 1972.

———. *Foxfire 2, 3,* and *4*. Garden City, N. Y.: Doubleday, 1973–77.

Wilkie, James W. *Elitelore*. Los Angeles: Latin American Center—University of California, 1973.

Williams, T. Harry. *Huey Long*. New York: Knopf, 1969.

Yessne, Peter. *Quotations from Mayor Daley*. New York: Putnam, 1969.